MW01505511

# CRYSTAL MAGIC

### Divination, Healing, and Spellcraft
### with
### Gems and Minerals

by

## Rev. Dr.
## JON SAINT GERMAIN

Author of

**Karmic Palmistry**
**Runic Palmistry**
**Palmistry for Lovers**

"The Voice of the Crystal Silence League"

Missionary Independent Spiritual Church
Forestville, California

❖ 2016 ❖

Crystal Magic:
Divination, Healing, and Spellcraft with Gems and Minerals
by Rev. Dr. Jon Saint Germain

© 2016 Jon Saint Germain
JonSaintGermain.com

Some of the material in this book appeared in draft form in
*The Crystal Gaze-ette*, the newsletter of
The Crystal Silence League
CrystalSilenceLeague.org

text:
Jon Saint Germain

Illustrations:
Nelson Hahne, S. Quinlan, B.C.S., Prof. Alfred F. Seward,
Unknown Arist, Jon Saint Germain, and Grey Townsend

Cover:
Grey Townsend and Unknown Arist for CSA-Images

editor:
catherine yronwode

Production:
nagasiva yronwode, Jon Saint Germain, and Grey Townsend

First Edition 2016

Published by
Missionary Independent Spiritual Church
6632 Covey Road
Forestville, California 95436
CandleMinistry.com

ISBN: 978-0-9960523-4-4

Printed in Canada.

# CONTENTS

# DEDICATION

Dedicated to the memory of Claude Alexander Conlin
Founder of the Crystal Silence League
Who passed into the Silence in 1954

# ACKNOWLEDGEMENTS

Thanks are due to many who assisted in the making of this book, especially Greywolf Townsend for art direction and nagasiva yronwode for book production. Thanks also to the staff of Missionary Independent Spiritual Church, and to catherine yronwode, Prof. Charles D. Porterfield, Miss Bri, Susan Diamond, Leah Rivera, Br. Jeffrey Vanderson, Dara Anzlowar, and Mother Mystic — the writers and editors of the Association of Independent Readers and Rootworkers who created AIRR's web pages on Crystal Gazing and New Thought — as well as to the Yronwode Institution for the Preservation and Popularization of Indigenous Ethnomagicology for YIPPIE's helpful online New Thought and Crystal Gazing bibliographies.

# INTRODUCTION

Some of the material in this book has appeared in abbreviated form in *The Crystal Gaze-ette,* the newsletter of the Crystal Silence League. I've expanded and developed it here to include a significant amount of information which didn't appear in the original publication. My goal when composing the newsletter articles was to feel my way toward tackling the monumental task of writing a full-length, comprehensive book about the work of a great man, one who passed into the Silence six years before I was born, whose literary legacy is enormous, and whose mastery of the techniques he taught unquestionable.

The goal of this book is to help further spread the work and ideas of Mr. Claude Conlin, and bring together in one resource some of the many spiritual and psychological techniques he adapted and developed. I've never liked long introductions, so as Mr. Conlin often wrote:

On to the Work!

Jon Saint Germain
Knoxville, Tennessee, January 2016

# CHAPTER ONE:
# THE CRYSTAL SILENCE LEAGUE

The Crystal Silence League came into existence around 1917, the vision of Claude Alexander Conlin, who created it for the purpose of distributing affirmative prayer and helpful thoughts to all in need.

Mr. Conlin received thousands of prayer requests via letters and postcards, and he prayed over great piles of them daily. Three times a day — morning, noon and night — Mr. Conlin Projected powerful and affirmative thoughts of health, joy, and mental soundness through his crystal ball, using it as a form of natural magnifying glass or mental amplifier, to reel out to all the members of the Crystal Silence League. The CSL members received these transmissions via similar crystal balls with which they were provided, and learned in turn how to pass the blessings on through their own crystal balls, to others in need.

Via Mr. Conlin's publications, members learned how to Project and Receive positive, healing affirmations, control the thoughts of others, and draw wealth and power into their grasp. It was a strange, wonderful, never-before-seen kind of ministry.

Throughout the 1920s, the Crystal Silence League grew into a large network of individuals joined together in a world-spanning communication system powered by concentrated mental effort, connected by crystal orbs. Mr. Conlin envisioned a worldwide web eighty years before the Internet!

Claude Alexander Conlin was born in Alexandria, South Dakota, in 1880. He travelled to Alaska for the Klondike Gold Rush, but did not strike it rich. While there, it is said that he saved the life of a young Greek American man named Pericles Pantages, who later took the name Alexander Pantages and went on to become the greatest theatrical and vaudeville impresario in the Western states. Claude Alexander Conlin gained enormous fame as the stage performer "Alexander, The Man Who Knows," between 1915 and 1924, playing at many of the Alexander Pantages theaters, and it is thought that these bookings were "Alexander" Pantages' way of repaying the debt he owed to "Alexander" Conlin.

Alexander's stage performance consisted of a magic show, followed by a clairvoyance demonstration where audience members submitted sealed questions, which he answered from the stage. At the height of his career, Alexander was the highest-paid performer in the world.

Alexander retired from the stage in 1927. Due to his private and reclusive nature, many details of his life remain a matter of speculation and mystery. It is known that he married, had a child, and settled in Los Angeles. Claude Conlin bequeathed us a rich literary legacy. In 1919 he launched the C. Alexander Publishing Company in Los Angeles to distribute his own astrological, Spiritualist, and New Thought writings, including a 5-volume series called *The Inner Secrets of Psychology.* He published instruction manuals for students: *Crystal Gazing,* and *Personal Lessons, Codes, and Instructions for Members of the Crystal Silence League,* which explained his Four Branches of crystal work, a unique system integrating crystallomancy with New Thought philosophy. Conlin also distributed the works of prominent New Thought and Spiritualist authors, notably William Walker Atkinson, who wrote under his own name and pseudonymously as Theron Q. Dumont, Yogi Ramacharaka, and Swami Panchadasi.

At its height, the Crystal Silence League was so popular that other spiritual workers imitated Conlin's methods. One brazen chap by the name of Mr. Clayton even to far as to create a create a copy-cat ministry which he called the Simla Silence League. (Simla is a town in India, but Clayton's group might just as well have been dubbed the Simulation Silence League.)

When Mr. Conlin passed into spirit in 1954, the Crystal Silence League passed with him. Fifty years later, few were left alive who still had their old crystal balls and manuals of affirmations, but in 2009, a group of Spiritual Adepts of the Missionary Independent Spiritual Church revived the Crystal Silence League online. You can find us at CrystalSilenceLeague.org.

Mr. Conlin assured his members:

*"… There is a way out of all your difficulties, I firmly believe. It consists of being able to make others think as you think, to project thoughts to others so they will have the effect you desire, and to control your own mind. You do not have to have beauty, physical strength, or wealth to do these things. YOU JUST HAVE TO BE WILLING TO HELP YOURSELF. This is an easy matter if you have the SECRET. And I firmly believe that CONCENTRATION WITH THE AID OF A CRYSTAL IS THE SECRET. It has been my success."*

It has been the success of many. If you've never practiced the techniques taught by Mr. Conlin, you're in for a rare new treat. The doors of a bright future are about to open for you!

But first, some background.

# CHAPTER TWO
# CRYSTALS, STONES, AND MINERALS

In the beginning, there was nothing. Not even vacuum. Vacuum requires space to exist, and in the beginning there wasn't even room enough for vacuum.

Then Consciousness emerged, which exists always outside Space and Time, and Consciousness Observed, bringing space and matter into existence. Then followed Expansion, a great flinging of this matter in every direction. Over vast eons, a tiny bit of this star-flung matter condensed, forming stars and planets, among them our own Earth, upon which we live and dream and die.

This story is told more poetically in Genesis, but my version seems appropriate for a book on crystals.

Matter was flung in every direction and some of it cooled, condensing into stars and planets. A wonderful thing! Rather than solidifying into a homogeneous chunk of rock, our Earth was a jewelry box, containing a nearly infinite variety of mineral compounds. Eventually we humans came along and began digging into the ground. Eventually, we discovered all these magical rocks, all shapes and colours, each with specific properties and potential uses. Since ancient times, these magical gifts of the earth have been used to heal and to hurt, to work magic, to create beautiful jewelry and art.

Imagine how amazing these sparkling stones must have been to ancient people — Rock Quartz especially, which looks like ice, but is warm! Brightly-coloured natural crystal gems seem to be shaped by unseen hands. Through a process of meditation and magical experimentation, stones and crystals have been integrated into religious rites and ceremonies, and people of every known culture recognize the magical qualities of these wondrous objects. They are obviously gifts from the Gods.

Crystals are born through restless geological forces constantly surging within the planet's interior. Forged in the crucible of the earth's fiery belly, crystals and minerals form as molten rock cools. Depending on pressures, speed of cooling, the chemistry of the materials in the molten compound, and many other factors, crystals grow into myriad forms. Some crystals are clear, some semi-transparent, and some completely opaque, and they come in every colour imaginable.

# WHAT'S THE DIFFERENCE BETWEEN CRYSTALS AND STONES?

Most crystal workers include healing stones, such as Calcite, Sodalite, Turquoise, and Lapis Lazuli under the umbrella term "crystals," even though they are more properly termed stones. This is just for convenience, like calling all carbonated beverages "colas" even though some aren't cola-based recipes. Yet, there is a difference.

Crystals "grow" in a repeating pattern called tessellations, often around a nucleus, while stones are an amalgam of minerals melded together. Crystals are minerals too, but instead of being melded in a homogeneous lump, the crystalline structure is repeated in a symmetrical pattern. This is easily seen in the larger crystals such as Quartz, Fluorite, and Pyrite, but it is not so obvious in a crystal such as Aventurine, which has such a small crystalline pattern you have to look through a microscope to see it.

Crystals also are not organic. Amber isn't a crystal, nor is it a stone. Coral isn't organic, but some consider it a stone because coral is almost pure calcium carbonate. Others do not, for the same reason Amber isn't: Coral is a product of living beings, not geological processes.

Obsidian is lava glass, so it isn't crystal, nor is it a stone. Obsidian is fused silicon dioxide — like most glass — and it is classed as a mineraloid.

Man-made crystals can be grown in laboratories, but they are not products of Nature and are seldom used for healing.

So the characteristics of crystals used for magical healing are:

- **Solid, not liquid at normal temperatures:** Mercury isn't a crystal.
- **Mineral, non-organic:** Sugar forms crystals, but it is not a mineral.
- **Naturally occurring:** For our purposes, cystals are not man-made.
- **Structurally comprised of tessellations:** They show a repeating pattern.

Stones tend to look like stones. Green Moss Agate couldn't be mistaken for a crystal, nor could Buddstone. There are exceptions, like Aventurine, which is hard to tell due to the small size of its crystals, but since stones are one or more minerals melded together, with no crystalline pattern, they tend to be roundish or lumpish and lack geometric shape. Some common stones used for healing and protection purposes are Calcite, Sodalite, Turquoise, Agate, Amethyst, Ocean Jasper, Jet, Tiger's Eye, Unakite, and Lapis Lazuli.

# SOME USEFUL THINGS TO KNOW

Working with crystals can be a very direct and personal spiritual experience, but you will learn faster if you absorb some basic knowledge.

## CRYSTAL WORKERS HAVE THEIR OWN TERMINOLOGY

As you meet other workers, you will hear them use these terms of art:

- **Crystals,** despite the technicality of the term, is a word often used interchangeably with stones; it can also refer to crystal balls or spheres.
- **Druse** is a natural coating of fine crystals on a rock fracture surface; druzy stones are those that are covered with tiny glittering crystals.
- **Gemstones** are hard, transparent stones suitable for jewelry; they may be cut into facets, smoothly domed cabochons, spherical beads, etc.
- **Geodes** are spherical and apparently solid stones, which, when broken open, are found to be hollow and coated with interior crystals.
- **Inclusions, Fractures, Vugs, and Rutilations** are imperfections in a stone. Some, like rutilations (included needles of Titanium Dioxide), are desirable; others, like vugs (crystal-lined cavities in polished pieces), are defects — unless you like their look, in which case they are assets.
- **Matrix** is a fine-grained mass of rock in which crystals are embedded.
- **Points** are crystals that form natural points, either single (at one end) or double (at both ends). Some examples are Quartz, Tourmaline, and Citrine. Artificial points are often carved in broken or imperfect crystals.
- **Roughs** are unworked pieces of stone; they are unpolished and irregular in form and size, just as they come from the rock mines.
- **Spheres** are crystal, glass, or stone balls, used to concentrate thoughts for divination; they are a form of worked stone.
- **Stones** can refer to both crystals and stones, as well as gemstones. You will often see the three terms used interchangeably.
- **Treated Stones** are those which have been variously bleached, dyed, irradiated, heated, or surface-coated to improve or change their colour.
- **Tumbles** are irregularly shaped stones that have been mechanically surface-polished by processing them in a rock tumbler machine.
- **Worked Stones** are stones that have been faceted, drilled as beads, or sculpted into forms such as hearts, disks, palm stones, or figural pieces.

## CRYSTALS AND STONES VARY IN HARDNESS

The relative hardness of stones is important to gemologists and jewellers. For instance, when tumbling stones, they must be of similar hardness; if you tumble soft Selenite with hard Quartz, you'll wear the Selenite down to pebbles. The Mohs Scale lists the hardness of minerals, and is useful for proper identification of stones which may look alike, such as Citrine Quartz and Imperial (Golden) Topaz. Knowledge of relative hardness is also helpful in magical works that call for stones of similar vibrational harmony.

## CRYSTALS HAVE MEMORY

All crystals and stones have some capacity to remember. They "learn" vibratory resonances as we work with them. We activate these resonances and the stone or crystal then radiates healing vibrations, or dissipates harmful spiritual energies, depending on what it has been taught to do.

The most common example of this principle is seen in works with Salt. Salt is blessed, cursed, prayed over, used for protection and cleansing — in fact, all manner of spells are worked with it. Folks often say, "Salt does what you tell it to." Conversely, Salt remembers what's been done to it.

Another example of mineral memory is found in the use of Lodestones. If a Lodestone has been named and trained to do a particular task, that is what it will do. A money Lodestone will rarely hunt for love, and a pair of mated love Lodestones will almost certainly not hunt for money, especially if the pair is broken up. That's why, if you no longer need a Lodestone's service, it's advised to "retire" it by burial in the earth with Magnetic Sand.

Crystals remember people, and can become attached to them. If you carry a touchstone for a long time, then give it to someone else, the stone may not work as well for them. It's become attuned to you. It remembers you. Sapphire is the best at this: if you wear one to ward off the evil eye, then lose it, the stone will continue to work for you wherever it is on Earth, as long as you live.

Not only can crystals be trained, the more they're used, the "smarter" they become. Clear Quartz can even temporarily imitate the properties of other crystals. For example, you can send a client home with a piece of Quartz programmed with the energy of an expensive crystal like Heliodor, to continue a healing process initiated in the office. The client can return every few days to "recharge" the Quartz with Heliodor, as needed.

## CRYSTALS CAN BE CLEANSED

Cleansing is a word you didn't hear with respect to crystals until the 1980s. The previous term was discharging. This meant releasing any negative energies your stones had absorbed during difficult healing sessions, similar to discharging a battery prior to taking on a new charge.

I mentioned above that stones have memory. It is common lore among crystal healers that stones store or "remember" bad experiences such as sessions with clients who carried heavy emotional burdens. When a stone becomes congested it must be discharged. I've known some workers who will retire a stone if it's absorbed too much stressful energy, but most professional crystal workers simply discharge their stones and crystals on a regular basis. In many cases, discharging also seems to recharge them.

- You can let the sun shine on them for a day.
- You can place them in running water for a day.
- You can bury them in the earth for a day.
- You can place crystal points in a bowl of Salt or uncooked rice.
- Selenite can be cleansed by exposing it to the moon's beams overnight.
- Citrine and Kyanite never need cleaning or discharging.
- Lodestones are fed by sprinkling them with Magnetic Sand.
- To wash your Lodestones, remove their Magnetic Sand, then bathe them in whiskey, Hoyt's Cologne, Florida Water, or any high-grade perfume.
- Stones that are weakly magnetic, such as Moqui Balls, can be recharged by resting overnight in a bowl of blessed Salt, between two Lodestones.
- Stones can be cleansed by rubbing them with Van Van Oil, smoking them in Uncrossing Incense, or performing Uncrossing work with them.
- You can smudge crystals with Frankincense, Sage, or Sweetgrass.
- To energize a weakened stone, hold it and send your own positive energies through it. This also "attunes" the stone to your personal touch.

## CRYSTALS ARE MAGNIFIERS

Cover your crystal balls when they are not in use. A clear sphere is a lens and can cause a fire. Petition papers set under uncovered crystals can start to smoulder in minutes. I'm serious. I once set my shirt on fire showing my large crystal to some friends at a psychic fair in Georgia on a hot summer day!

## CRYSTALS ARE FORGIVING

One of the best things about working with crystals is that it's hard to go wrong. You're not going to harm yourself through the improper use of a crystal. You just may not get the results you desired. You can always recover and try again. It's like learning to play the piano. You may not get the song you tried to play, but at least you get to make noise and have fun.

## CRYSTALS HAVE PERSONALITY

As you work with them, you will find that each crystal has its own unique character. Sunstone is open, honest, and vibrant. Obsidian is contemplative, mysterious, and introverted. Like cats, even within the species, each stone is different. No two pieces of Rose Quartz are the same, for example. That's why it's important to select your crystal toolkit carefully. Some stones may feel better to you than others. You'll connect with one piece of Quartz while another does nothing for you. If possible, go to a rock shop where you can handle the stones and find those that resonate with you.

You may find that you have a natural affinity for certain minerals. Some people like to work with their birthstone, or stones associated with certain planets. Some like smooth stones; others enjoy textured surfaces. Colour plays a role, as well. Orange stones have a different "feel" — a different personality — than blue or green stones. Over time, you can even learn to distinguish the different energy signatures between two seemingly identical stones of the same colour, based solely on the "memory" stored within them.

Selecting a stone is much like adopting a pet. It selects you every bit as much as you select it. Rocks and crystals are living things, birthed by the living earth. They respond to touch, and they remember your touch. This is why we can work such wonderful magic with their assistance.

It's important to enter into a respectful relationship with your stone and understand its nature. Connecting with your stone is a process you can learn quickly. Hold the stone in your hand and curl your fingers around it. Take a few deep breaths, centering your thoughts into the stone, feeling for its energy center. The stone will warm to your touch, and you may feel a low throbbing. Speak to the stone, either silently or out loud, asking for its assistance. Listen for its response. It may not answer in words, but in feelings or images. There should be a "click," a coming together, a sense of connection.

## CRYSTALS MAY BE PARTNERED WITH OTHER CRYSTALS

As with herbs or roots which are mingled in making a mojo hand, compounded in a conjure oil, or blended together in a medicinal tea, minerals also can be mixed for effective working.

Some crystal combinations are based on the mineralogical qualities of the stones. For example, colourful Quartzes like Citrine, Amethyst, Ametrine, Rose Quartz, Smoky Quartz, Lemon Quartz, and Prasiolite have similar hardness and reflectivity, so they work well together as a grouping of same-sized stones. Likewise, a matched set of coloured Beryl crystals like Red Beryl, Morganite, Golden Beryl, Heliodor, Emerald, and Aquamarine, although very costly, would prove exceptionally harmonious as gems.

Combinations may also be based on colour symbolism. If you perform a money attraction with dark green Malachite, for example, you may include golden Citrine for business success and light green Aventurine for luck.

We'll take a closer look at how to combine naturally coloured stones with coloured glass crystal balls in Chapter Seven.

## SOME CRYSTALS ARE KNOWN AS "ANGEL STONES"

"Angel Stones" are minerals that facilitate communication with Angels, Archangels, and dwellers in other dimensions. These stones are:

- **Angelite**   • **Celestite**   • **Danburite** • **Galaxite**   • **Iolite**
- **Labradorite** • **Larimar**   • **Morganite** • **Selenite**   • **Seraphinite**

It's said that meditating while holding or wearing one or more of these Angel Stones can open one up to awareness of higher consciousness.

## SOME CRYSTALS ARE "OUT OF THIS WORLD"

Meteorites are stony or metallic minerals that have come to Earth from outer space. Moldavite and Tektite are the remains of sandy detritus thrown upward when an ancient meteor stuck, which then fell to Earth as fused glass.

- **Meteorite**      • **Moldavite**      • **Tektite**

These otherworldly stones help to connect us with the Outer Realms.

# YOU CAN SELECT CRYSTALS FOR SPECIFIC CONDITIONS

Here are some common life conditions and the stones that address them:

- **Animal Totem:** Leopard Skin Jasper, Snakeskin Agate, Serpentine.
- **Addiction:** Apatite, Iolite, Unakite, Xenotime, Tibetan Quartz.
- **Athleticism:** Bloodstone, Carnelian, Smoky Quartz.
- **Blessing:** Angelite, Celestite, Danburite, and other Angel Stones.
- **Clarity:** Fuchsite, Sodalite, Kunzite, Clear Quartz, White Jade.
- **Communication:** Blue Lace Agate, Chrysocolla, Turquoise.
- **Courage:** Aquamarine, Charoite, Ruby, Hematite, Garnet.
- **Court Cases:** Malachite, Heliodor, Blue Apatite, Copper, Hematite.
- **Depression:** Peridot, Smoky Quartz, Blue Topaz, Amethyst, Quartz.
- **Fidelity:** Lapis Lazuli, Blue Tourmaline, Opal, Amethyst, Emerald.
- **Friendship:** Carnelian, Lapis Lazuli, Almandine, Turquoise.
- **Gambling:** Aventurine, Pyrite, Yellow Scapolite, Lodestone.
- **Happy Home:** Blue Lace Agate, Clear Quartz, Sugilite.
- **Healing:** Heliodor, Sunstone, Ruby in Kyanite, Ruby in Fuchsite, Rose Quartz, Garnet, Agate, Carnelian, Turquoise.
- **Love Attracting:** Rose Quartz, Pink Kyanite, Ruby, Rhodochrosite, Rhodonite, Morganite, Manganocalcite, Emerald, Paired Lodestones.
- **Love Uncrossing:** Chalcedony, Dioptase, Neptunite.
- **Luck:** Amazonite, Aventurine, Sunstone, Lodestone, Fluorite, Pyrite.
- **Magic:** Merlinite, Nuumite, Selenite, Isis Calcite.
- **Money and Prosperity:** Pyrite, Lodestone, Watermelon Tourmaline, Green Aventurine, Citrine, Yellow Scapulite, Malachite, Peridot.
- **Necromancy:** Nuumite, Moonstone, Celestine, Jet.
- **Protection:** Black Tourmaline, Holed Stones, Ocean Jasper, Picture Jasper, Eye Agate, Tiger's Eye, Carnelian, Sapphire, Jet, Jade, Ruby.
- **Psychic Vision:** Iolite, Isis Calcite, Azurite, Nebula Stone.
- **Reconciliation:** Chrysocholla, Dioptase, Larimar, Rose Quartz.
- **Road Opening:** Kunzite, Orange Kyanite, Picture Jasper, Serpentine.
- **Sexual Potency:** Fire Opal, Almandine, Red Tourmaline.
- **Sleep:** Amethyst, Muscovite, Rose Quartz, Lepidolite, Galaxite.
- **Tranquility:** Amethyst, Howlite, Lepidolite, Moss Agate, Chrysoprase.
- **Uncrossing:** Black Obsidian, Rutilated Quartz, Green Tourmaline.
- **Wisdom:** Jade, Lapis Lazuli, Black Obsidian, Black Onyx.

Crystal Balls offered for sale in catalogues, 1916 - 1956. Art by Nelson Hahne, "B.C.S.," Professor A. F. Seward, S. Quinlan, and One Unknown Artist for Oracle Products Co., Nelson Enterprises, Psychic Sciences Co., and A. F. Seward & Co.

# CHAPTER THREE
# A COLLECTION OF CRYSTALS FROM A TO Z

Though far from exhaustive, the following list provides a reasonable sampling of crystals and stones suitable for most of life's situations. It is not a complete encyclopedia of every crystal, stone, mineral, or mineraloid available to the crystal worker, and it also includes a few non-mineral substances with a long history of use in gemstone jewelry.

Throughout the list, references are made to the Asian system of Chakras on the body; see Chapter Seven for a full explanation of how this works.

Likewise, references to the classical European system indicating which stones symbolize which signs of the Zodiac are amplified in Chapter Nine.

Finally, other aspects of a stone — its colour, hardness, manner of reflectivity, or figuring, may help determine its traditional uses.

• **Abalone:** This is the peacock-hued inner shell of the Abalone mollusk. (Other mollusk species produce paler material known as Mother of Pearl.) It has a soothing effect in emotionally volatile situations, promotes psychic awareness, and enhances creative development, Its rainbow sheen harmonizes with the Root, Sacral, and Brow or Third Eye Chakra.

• **Agate:** Agate is a stone of Gemini that comes in a variety of colours: clear, pink, rose, purple, black, yellow, orange, tan, brown, green, or blue. The properties of Agate vary depending on colour, but be aware that Agate can be dyed and some workers prefer only the natural colours.

• **Agate, Banded:** Any Agate with wavy layers of colour is called "banded." Available in white, cream, tan, brown, grey, blue, green, or other hues, each stone's colouring determines its metaphysical properties.

• **Agate, Blue Lace:** Resonating with the Throat Chakra, Blue Lace Agate encourages peaceful, sensitive communication, especially when worn by a man. It's said to bring Yin (female) energy into balance with Yang (male). It promotes calm, positive, and joyful relations, and facilitates harmony.

• **Agate, Botswana:** Stimulating the Root Chakra, Botswana Agate, with its eye-like formations, resembles a protective eye. It can help alleviate obsessive and addictive behaviour, and many healers recommend it as an aid for smoking cessation and weight reduction.

• **Agate, Eye:** A striped Agate cut and worked to create eye-like disks, this stone protects against and repels the evil eye or the eye of envious attacks.

• **Agate, Moss:** An "earthy" and protective stone, Moss Agate connects us to Nature. Associated with the Heart Chakra, it provides strength and fortitude during trying times and aid in recovery from illness, exhaustion, or trauma.

• **Alabaster:** Fine-grained Gypsum (European Alabaster) and fine-grained Calcite (Egyptian Alabaster) are easy to carve and are worked into sacred statuary, bowls, amulets, and fetishes. White Alabaster symbolizes purity.

• **Alexandrite:** A rare form of Chrysoberyl, Alexandrite is greenish in daylight and reddish under incandescent light. It balances emotions and actions.

• **Amazonite:** Bright blue-green Amazonite works between the Heart and Throat Chakras to aid compassionate communication, mediating between intuition and analytic thought. As "the Stone of Hope," it grants strength and optimism to those seek to bring people together during trying times.

• **Amber:** Neither a stone nor a crystal, Amber is fossilized tree resin, and retains a strong connection to Nature and earth energies. Attributed to Leo, it promotes courage, protects the wearer from harm, and strengthens the soul. If an insect is preserved in a piece, it's valued for its protective properties.

• **Amethyst:** Purple Amethyst supports the Third Eye Chakra. Place it under your pillow to relieve nightmares and enhance clairvoyant dreams. It protects against poison, removes fear, dispels negativity, and aids concentration. It is a stone of Pisces. Druzy Amethyst points are called Cactus or Spirit Quartz.

• **Ametrine:** Heating Amethyst turns it into Citrine; if it is partially heated, beautiful crystals flashing both purple and golden-yellow are the result. Ametrine blends the protective qualities of Amethyst with the prosperity-drawing qualities of Citrine, making it the perfect money-stay-with-me gem.

• **Angelite:** One of the Angel Stones, Angelite strengthens connection to Higher Powers and ethereal spiritual energies. It can produce a feeling of peace and contentment, and used in Chakra work to clear energy blockages.

• **Almandine:** This common red to reddish-brown Garnet works with the Root Chakra to ground and resolve insecurities in matters of food, shelter, and employment. It boosts the libido and promotes health, trust, power, passion, and friendship. It can assist in the practice of Kundalini yoga.

• **Apatite:** From cyan to blue, Apatite eases emotional turmoil, promotes tranquility, provides confidence in love, and helps in matters of addiction, especially eating disorders. It protects the heart from emotional assault.

• **Aquamarine:** "The Stone of Courage," sea-blue Aquamarine is a Scorpio stone. worn for protection, to give the bearer fortitude, to enhance intuition, and to ward off magical assault. A form of Beryl, it is a great scrying stone.

• **Aragonite:** Brown Aragonite crystal clusters connect to the Root and Earth Chakras and are employed by conservationists to protect wild Nature. Healers who work to relieve geopathic stress also use them to clear blocked ley lines.
• **Aventurine:** Aventurine eases the pain of heartache and loss, granting respite to a troubled mind. Sleep with it under your pillow to wake up with insights to perplexing problems. Green Aventurine is used in money charms and spells; Cinnamon Aventurine supports the Sacral Chakra and sexuality.
• **Beryl:** Beryl comes in several colours: Red Beryl, pink Morganite, yellow Golden Beryl, yellow-green Heliodor, green Emerald, and pale-blue Aquamarine. It has the reputation for being the best of all the scrying stones.
• **Bloodstone:** Dark green with Red Jasper inclusions, Bloodstone supports the Heart Chakra and is a stone of Aries. It banishes negativity and anger; promotes courage, determination, and good health; wards off snake bite; and heals illness, especially conditions involving the circulatory system.
• **Calcite:** Available in colours ranging from almost-clear Iceland Spar, through White or Isis Calcite, to Honey and Orange Calcite, this is a great stone for beginners learning to scry, and is said to improve the memory.
• **Calcite, Isis:** With a strong link to the Sacred Feminine, snow-white Isis Calcite is a Crown Chakra stone that enhances latent psychic abilities.
• **Carnelian:** This sunny Virgo stone aids the Sacral Chakra, for a grounding, energizing, and revitalizing effect. It can restore and recharge a sluggish metabolism and boost a flagging sex drive, plus it works in prosperity spells.
• **Celestite:** One of the Angel Stones, grey-blue Strontium Sulfate or Celestite is a Crown Chakra stone that aids contact with Angels, facilitates meditation, and brings feelings of peace and "oneness" with all creation.
• **Chalcedony:** Waxy, lustrous, and translucent, Chalcedony comes in white, grey, blue, green, and brown. It heals old emotional and physical wounds. Blue Chalcedony absorbs negativity by diffusing anger and resentment.
• **Charoite:** This violet-purple stone lends strength during times of adversity, loneliness, isolation, and unemployment. It supports the Crown Chakra with objectivity, detachment, and insight. It is prized for Violet Flame work.
• **Cat's-Eye:** Chatoyant Apatite, Chrysoberyl, Quartz, and Sillimanite Cat's-Eyes repel the evil eye and bring success in business and gambling. Stones of Cancer, they aid the Heart or Solar Plexus Chakra, depending on their tints.
• **Chrysocolla:** This cyan-blue stone is reputed to smooth over difficulties in troubled relationships eases emotional heartache and remorse. Sitting with Chrysocolla in meditation can help kindle insights into yourself and others.

- **Chrysoprase:** During healing work on burnt-out energies and tired spirits, Chrysoprase, an apple-green form of Chalcedony, brings new beginnings and childlike joy to the Heart Chakra when most needed. It is a stone of Gemini.
- **Citrine:** Citrine Quartz harmonizes with the Solar Plexus Chakra. An aid to business prosperity and abundance, Citrine can also recharge flagging enthusiasm or cool off over-assertive pushiness. This yellow-gold stone never needs cleansing, making it particularly prized among crystal workers.
- **Coral:** While not a stone, Red Coral is used as such in amulets. Sacred to the goddess Venus, it protects against evil, and heals the blood and kidneys.
- **Danburite:** Danburite, an Angel Stone, is clear or subtly tinted pink; it aids the Crown or Heart Chakra in communion with Higher Powers.
- **Diamond:** The hardest gem, it is a stone of Aries. Its ancient Greek name was "adamas" or "invincible." It radiates purity, perfection, and permanence.
- **Dioptase:** This rare green crystal has a powerful vibratory connection to the Heart Chakra. It is wonderful for dramatic mental and emotional healing, specifically regarding past relationship issues or childhood trauma.
- **Emerald:** This precious green Beryl is sacred to the goddess Venus and the sign of Cancer. It stimulates love, confers wisdom and mercy, and strengthens the heart. Expense notwithstanding, it is a favoured scrying stone in India.
- **Flint:** A common grey stone, Flint can be used for making arrowheads, will spark a fire when two pieces are hit together, and it is a good scrying stone.
- **Fluorite:** Fluorite or Fluorspar's distinctive cubical crystals mingle shades of emerald-green and purple. It is a stone of mental order and truthfulness.
- **Fuchsite:** Fuchsite cuts through confusion, so you can develop objectivity and access practical knowledge. Pale green, it is a Heart Chakra stone.
- **Galaxite:** A dramatic blend of sparkly micro-crystals of Labradorite in a black Feldspar matrix, this Angel stone, which looks like a photograph of deep space, reduces fear, and helps to end bad dreams or nightmares.
- **Garnet:** Pyrope, Almandine, and Spessartine are Red Garnets, also known as Carbuncle. Harmonizing with the Root Chakra, they enhance stability and trust in relationships, giving a sense of security, personal power, and strength.
- **Healers Gold:** This natural mix of yellowish Pyrite and blackish Iron Magnetite is used to heal money issues, to assist healers to heal themselves, and to balance the passive and assertive aspects of one's natural personality.
- **Heliodor:** A yellow-green Beryl, Heliodor resonates with the Solar Plexus Chakra, radiating joy, hope, optimism, energy, and positivity, and banishing gloom and dejection. Like all of the Beryls, it is an excellent scrying stone.

• **Hematite:** A powerful grounding stone, Hematite or Iron Oxide vibrates to the Root and Earth Chakras. It deflects negative spiritual energies, and, like Lodestone, it can be trained to attract prosperity, love, and popularity.

• **Holed Rock:** Also called Holey or Holy Stones, Hag Stones, Adder Stones, Serpent's Eggs, or Witch Stones, naturally holed rocks protect against evil, bring second sight, and are said to assist in healing the body.

• **Howlite:** Serenity-inducing grey-veined white Howlite absorbs residual anger and resentment. Howlite is often dyed to mimic Turquoise or Coral.

• **Hyacinth:** Orange Hyacinth is a variety of Zircon associated with the astrological sign of Aquarius, It is a Sacral Chakra stone of sexuality.

• **Iolite:** As an Angel Stone in tune with the Third Eye, blue-violet Iolite assists psychic development and uproots addictive and destructive behaviours.

• **Jade:** From white and pale green to dark green and black, sacred, lustrous Jadeite and Nephrite bring blessings, good luck, long life, and a peaceful death. A stone of Virgo, Jades toughness is protective and health-giving.

• **Jacinth:** Reddish-brown Jacinth is a form of Zircon. A stone of Aquarius, it protects from danger, theft, and witchcraft, and helps to end harmful habits.

• **Jasper:** The properties of the various Jaspers depend on their colour, but all Jaspers are calming, nurturing, protective, and relaxing to carry or wear.

• **Jasper, Brown:** Allied with the Root Chakra and the life force, Brown Jasper supports people with chronic illness as well as those in rehabilitation.

• **Jasper, Chohua:** Also called Chinese Painting Jasper, this stone restores honour, connects us to ancestors, and is said to aid those with skin disorders.

• **Jasper, Franciscan:** A brecciated mix of cream-white and brownish-red, Franciscan Jasper promotes peace and facilitates acceptance of others.

• **Jasper, Kambaba:** Fossilized stromatolite algæ, a green stone with black orbicular markings, it fosters plant growth; set pieces in your potted plants.

• **Jasper, Leopard Skin:** Sit in meditation with a piece of this mottled stone and commune with your animal totem. If you're patient, it will help you.

• **Jasper, Ocean:** Ocean Jasper's circular patterns look like protective eyes, keeping away negative energies and psychic attack from the evil eye.

• **Jasper, Picasso:** Striated and streaked Picasso Jasper gets its name from art and is reputed to inspire creativity and stimulate out-of-the-box thinking.

• **Jasper, Picture:** Picture Jasper heals old emotional wounds and banishes unfounded fears. Its ancestral call reminds us to be responsible for the Earth.

• **Jasper, Red:** Allied with the Root Chakra, Red Jasper helps with issues of greed, fear, injustice, addiction, insecurities, and the need for protection.

• **Jet:** A fossilized driftwood, Jet is light in weight but black in colour. A stone of Capricorn, it represents mourning. Its lustrous surface is used for scrying.

• **Kunzite:** A Heart Chakra stone, pink Kunzite promotes unconditional love and the giving and receiving of affection. Its gentle nature is especially good for babies and children; place a small piece of it under the mattress.

• **Kyanite:** Blue Kyanite is a Throat Chakra stone that facilitates spiritual and verbal communication. Black Kyanite is a grounding agent. Kyanite, like Citrine, never needs cleansing, simply carrying it is beneficial for your aura.

• **Labradorite:** One of the Angel Stones, sparkling Labradorite resonates with the Third Eye Chakra and facilitates communication with Other Realms. It cleans the aura of negative or "dirty" energy picked up from other people.

• **Lapis Lazuli:** Lapis Lazuli opens the Third Eye to initiate spiritual awakening, astral travel, and enlightenment. Pyrite inclusions provide a protective and prosperous aspect, shielding the wearer from attack.

• **Larimar:** Also known as Atlantis Stone or Stefilia's Stone, blue Larimar resonates with the Throat Chakra to reveal difficult truths — especially healing truths which relieve emotional burdens and release old secrets.

• **Lepidolite:** A powerful stress relieving stone, sparkly lavender Lepidolite stills the hyper-active, worried mind and eases deep-rooted anxieties.

• **Limestone:** Limestone is a sedimentary Earth Chakra stone. It often forms beautiful cave structures. One variety, Travertine, is found around hot springs.

• **Lodestone:** Naturally magnetic Magnetite, a form of Iron ore, Lodestone is associated with the astrological sign of Scorpio. Due to its magnetism, it is used in both love-drawing and money-drawing spells. To keep it working, Lodestone is fed with Magnetic Sand or Anvil Dust.

• **Malachite:** Resonating with the Heart Chakra, green Malachite is a stone of Capricorn. It helps prevent romantic self-sabotage by promoting better "love sense" and discouraging involvement with the wrong type of partner. As a symbol of wealth and abundance, it's also used in money spells and charms.

• **Merlinite:** Merlinite, the Magician's Stone, is a mix of white Chalcedony and black Manganese Oxide. Unlocking access to the Akashic Records, it is used as a scrying tool and in meditation to promote mystical experiences.

• **Meteorite:** Both stony and metallic Meteorites from outer space are prized. Iron Meteorites worked into tools or worn as amulets are particularly potent.

• **Moonstone:** Resonating with the Soul Chakra, Moonstone, with its gentle, feminine energy, Moonstone strengthens intuition, promotes spiritual awakening, and enhances clairvoyant dreams.

• **Moqui Marbles:** Also known as Moqui Balls, Shaman Stones, or Boji Balls, these weakly magnetic Iron-coated Sandstone spheres help in training for psychism, in astral vision quests, and when contacting animal spirits.

• **Moldavite:** A glassy, fern-like, mossy-green Tektite formed by a meteoric impact, this rare stone facilitates communication with Extraterrestrial Realms.

• **Morganite:** A pink Beryl and an Angel Stone, Morganite facilitates connection and communication with the Angelic Realm, Higher Powers, and other-dimensional beings. It supports the Heart Chakra and eases the pain of separation. It's said to help with eating disorders and emotional attachments.

• **Muscovite:** Translucent Muscovite, also known as Mica or Isinglass, relieves troubled sleep, clears mental confusion, and helps those with dyslexia and that strange form of left / right confusion from which many people suffer.

• **Nebula Stone:** Consisting of a black matrix with small green orbicules, this is a grounding and protective stone associated with the Root Chakra. It helps with memory of all kinds, including past-life recall.

• **Neptunite:** Glassy black Neptunite, attuned to the Root Chakra, helps cool down emotions so that anger and passion can be expressed appropriately. It also provides protection during any activity involving water.

• **Nuummite:** Resonating with the Earth Chakra, black Nuummite, with its streaks of sparkling gold and cyan inclusions, assists in shamanic and natural magic. It is also excellent for protection against magical attacks.

• **Obsidian:** A naturally occurring volcanic glass, Obsidian works with the Root Chakra. It is grounding and protective. Nothing absorbs negativity like Obsidian. It can be worked by knapping to make arrows and knife blades.

• **Obsidian, Black:** Black Obsidian provides powerful protection from psychic attack. It helps in cutting attachments from harmful people, places, or habits. Due to its deep, shiny surface Obsidian is excellent for scrying.

• **Obsidian, Mahogany:** A mixture of earthy brown and deep black makes protective Mahogany Obsidian particularly useful for connecting to the Earth. It is also said to help break limitations and expand boundaries.

• **Obsidian, Rainbow:** Rainbow Obsidian has a faint rainbow sheen that lifts the spirits and brings light into the darkest situation, promoting levity, hope, and a childlike joy where it's most needed. It is excellent for scrying.

• **Obsidian, Snowflake:** Glossy black, with scattered grey "snowflakes" of Cristobalite all over, Snowflake Obsidian brings to the surface that which is hidden. It reveals issues that need resolution and provides the stability required to resolve them. It's a terrific stone for psychological healing.

• **Onyx:** Onyx, a form of banded Chalcedony, comes in black, white, gray, blue, brown, yellow, and red. It provides solid emotional support to the bearer during stressful times. Some workers access past life memories by placing an Onyx at the base of the skull. Black Onyx is a stone of Capricorn.

• **Opal:** Opal eases transitions from one state of being to another. It can bring to the surface deeply-buried feelings and memories, and discharge strong negativity. Fire Opal is lucky, but White Opal is unlucky in an engagement ring and useless to those who are selfish. Black Opal is a stone of witchcraft.

• **Opal, Fire:** In harmony with the Root and Sacral Chakras, multicoloured Fire Opal or Girasol restores optimism and enthusiasm while it banishes boredom and despair. A stone of Libra, it increases hope and productivity.

• **Peacock Ore:** Also known as Bornite or Chalcopyrite, this iridescent blue and purple metallic mineral brings happiness and joy. It is said to help rid the body of toxins and infections, and some say it even stimulates hair growth.

• **Pearl:** Formed within the shell of a mollusk, the Pearl is not a stone, but is used similarly; attributed to Cancer, it is a powerful self-healer for women.

• **Petrified Wood:** A good stone for grounding and protection in business matters, Petrified Wood is calming to those who are anxious about the future.

• **Peridot:** Yellow-green Peridot or Olivine is a Heart Chakra stone that mends emotional hurts. Leo's stone, it helps us understand relationships, especially the ones that didn't work out, so we can release them without pain.

• **Prasiolite:** A pale green Quartz, related to Amethyst and Citrine, Prasiolite fosters prosperity, wards off intoxication, and brings good fortune and luck

• **Pyrite:** Often used in money spells, metallic golden Pyrite placed in a cash register attracts customers to a place of business. It is protective, resonates with the Solar Plexus Chakra, and enhances intelligence, logic, and wealth.

• **Pyrope:** This is the less common, but most-loved form of pomegranate-red Garnet. Traditionally known as Bohemian Garnet, its small crystals are used in amuletic women's jewelry to increase love, sexuality, and female power.

• **Quartz:** Quartz is undoubtedly the most versatile crystal on the planet. In addition to Clear, Milky, Smoky, Spirit, Rose, Rutilated, and other colourful Quartzes, its forms include a number of stones that bear their own traditional names, such as Amethyst, Ametrine, Aventurine, Citrine, and Prasiolite.

• **Quartz, Clear and Milky:** Clear Quartz is said to draw out negativity. It can store, amplify, restructure, focus, transmit and transform energy. A spiritual Chameleon, it can be programmed to temporarily mimic the qualities of any other crystal. Milky Quartaz is similar to Clear, but less intensely energetic.

• **Quartz, Harlequin:** Rusty Harlequin or Ferruginous Quartz is a re-energizer, filling tired spirits with vitality. It resonates with the Root Chakra.
• **Quartz, Lithium:** Tinged by Lithium and other minerals, these pale pink crystals are used, as medical Lithium is, to soothe and calm mental distress.
• **Quartz, Rose:** Rose Quartz is the crystal associated with love. It is incorporated into a great many love charms, spells, and amulets. It resonates with the Heart Chakra, so it's useful for working with issues involving compassion, empathy, trust, acceptance of self and others, and loving freely.
• **Quartz, Rutilated:** Clear Quartz with needle-like inclusions of Rutile, this energizing stone is believed to stabilize rocky love relationships, balance and energize the aura, and tease out hidden reserves of energy and knowledge.
• **Quartz, Smoky:** A "negativity sponge," Smoky Quartz must be discharged often. It absorbs negative energies, and the darker the crystal, the better.
• **Quartz, Strawberry:** A formidable Heart Chakra crystal, Strawberry Quartz, with its red Iron Oxide inclusions, helps forge a link between the soul and its Creator, aiding investigation into the deeper questions of existence.
• **Quartz, Tibetan:** Resonating with the Crown Chakra, Tibetan Quartz is said to hold the "Om" vibration. The clear crystals contain black carbon inclusions, and when placed in a healing grid, they break up blocked energy.
• **River Rock:** Polished by natural tumbling processes in rivers and streams, River Rocks can be of almost any composition, but most are light or dark tan, grey, or grey-blue. They are used for connection to the Earth Chakra.
• **Ruby:** Red Corundum or Ruby works with the Root Chakra. A stone of Capricorn, it increases the life-force or chi, stimulates flagging libido, attracts new love, rekindles passion in a fading relationship, and energizes creativity.
• **Ruby in Kyanite:** Dark red Ruby in blue Kyanite supports the Throat Chakra and assist both physical vocalization and the speaking of truth.
• **Ruby in Fuchsite:** Dark pink Ruby in green Fuchsite makes a fine healers' massage wand and ball set to break up Heart Chakra blockages. It aids the circulatory system and combines love with prosperity.
• **Rutile:** Rutiles are needle-like crystals of Titanium Dioxide, often tinged with the golden or brown tones of Iron. They promote spiritual and emotional healing and are most prized by workers when found as inclusions in Quartz.
• **Sapphire:** From blue and green through yellow and orange, Sapphire or Corundum is a stone of Taurus. It brings wisdom and protects from envy.
• **Sapphire, Star:** A rare form of Sapphire, its six-rayed star is comprised of tiny needles of Rutile. It confers clarity and prophetic gifts upon the wearer.

• **Sardonyx:** Sardonyx is comprised of a layer of lustrous White Chalcedony or Sard atop a layer of reddish-brown Carnelian or Onyx. A stone of Leo, it has been used since ancient times for the carving of magical cameos.

• **Selenite:** Soft Gypsum, also known as Satin Spar, shimmery-white Selenite is a stone of Cancer, the Crown Chakra, and the moon; it absorbs negativity,

• **Septarian:** A fractured-and-melded mix of yellow Calcite, grey Limestone brown Aragonite, and clear Barite, Septarian is calming and nurturing. It helps mends the hearts of those have lost love in a break-up or through death.

• **Seraphinite:** An Angel Stone, Seraphinite assists Angelic contacts, upholds the Third Eye Chakra, and aids clairvoyance, clairaudience, and psychism.

• **Serpentine:** This name applies to several different mottled or streaked green and black stones. All of them open blocked paths and help raise Kundalini.

• **Shattuckite:** Bright peacock-blue, this stone fosters the development of psychic visions, mediumship, channeling, intuition, and automatic writing.

• **Shiva Linga Stone:** These red-brown and grey striped and spotted stones from the Narmada River in India are sacred to the Hindu god Shiva. Hand polished to a smooth rounded shape, they promote love, peace, and fertility.

• **Soapstone:** Also known as Steatite, this soft Talc-Schist is easily carved into cups, bowls, statuary, seals, amulets, fetishes, and other sacred goods.

• **Sodalite:** Blue and white Sodalite resonates with the Third Eye Chakra and helps with clarity, focus, calming, meditation, insight, and analytical thought.

• **Spinel:** Available in blue, green, yellow, red, brown, or black, Spinel is called "The Great Impostor," for although red Spinels convey fine confidence and leadership, they were often sold falsely as Rubies in times past.

• **Sugilite:** Red-violet Sugilite resonates to the Crown Chakra, and is one of the Violet Flame stones. As such, it is a powerful healing crystal.

• **Sunstone:** Cheerful Sunstone is a peachy-spangled Feldspar that lifts tired spirits and restores depleted energies. Sustaining the Solar Plexus Chakra, it it is carried or worn to bring in prosperity, love, luck, vitality, and success.

• **Tanzanite:** A rare, purplish-blue gemstone, it activates several Chakras from the Crown down to the Heart and is used to link the mind with serenity.

• **Tektite:** Tektites are blackish glass lumps formed when terrestrial debris is ejected during meteorite impacts. They are used as talismans during astral travel and shamanic journeying, as fertility charms, and to convey good luck.

• **Tiger's Eye**: Supporting the Solar Plexus Chakra, yellow-brown streaked and chatoyant Tiger's Eye is protective and brings strength, courage, fortune, and luck. Spheres or palm stones of Tiger's Eye make fine scrying surfaces.

• **Tiger Iron:** Tiger's Eye banded with Hematite and Red Jasper is known as Tiger Iron; it gives the courage to live a life of mental and emotional integrity.

• **Topaz:** Topaz, a stone of truth, ranges in hue from clear to red, pink, gold, orange, yellow, and blue. A stone of Sagittarius, its qualities vary by colour.

• **Topaz, Blue:** Heavenly Blue Topaz works with the Throat Chakra to aid communication, end writer's block, and enhance the power of speech. It may be worn as jewelry by those who speak before the public.

• **Topaz, Imperial:** Golden Imperial Topaz works with the Sacral Chakra and the astrological sign of Leo to catalyze manifestation. Wear it to materialize your desires and make your dreams come true.

• **Tourmaline:** The qualities of Tourmaline vary depending on colour, but all Tourmalines are powerful protective crystals and resonate to the sign of Leo.

• **Tourmaline, Black:** A Root Chakra stone, inky Black Tourmaline or Schorl is prized for its ability to reverse back every form of spiritual, physical, environmental, verbal, and magical attack.

• **Tourmaline, Blue:** Attuned to the Third Eye Chakra, Blue Tourmaline or Indicolite is believed to help achieve higher spiritual awareness.

• **Tourmaline, Green:** Resonating with the Heart Chakra, Green Tourmaline or Verdelite helps with grief, despair, loss, despondency, or depression.

• **Tourmaline, Pink:** A Heart Chakra stone, Pink Tourmaline or Rubellite heals losses, broken relationships, childhood hurts, and emotional betrayals.

• **Tourmaline, Watermelon:** A half-pink and half-green Heart Chakra stone, this cheerful little gem synchronizes our hopes for money and for love.

• **Tsavorite:** This is a rare bright green Garnet, associated with the power of wealth-getting and reputed to be of aid to those with failing eyesight.

• **Turquoise:** A stone of Taurus and the Throat Chakra, blue-green Turquoise enhances communication and protects those who express difficult truths. Native Americans believe Turquoise warns the bearer of impending danger. It is widely used in jewelry and amulets.

• **Unakite:** Mottled green and pink, Unakite Jasper resonates with the Heart Chakra. It assists with issues of smoking and overeating, can help with conception, and, like Watermelon Tourmaline, it is incorporated into spells or amulets that combine work for both prosperity and love.

• **Uvarovite:** An intensely green druzy Garnet, Uvarovite is a Heart Chakra stone that awakens compassion and universal love. Like most green crystals, it is used in money spells, but with a twist, for it fosters the wealth of non-profit charities.

• **Victorite:** Pink Spinel in a matrix of sparkly black Biotite Mica Schist, Victorite bridges from the Root to the Crown Chakra. A versatile stone, it is used in Chakra wands as well as healers' massage wand and ball sets.

• **Variscite:** Resonating to the Heart Chakra, green mottled and veined Variscite provides emotional stability and calm courage.

• **Vesuvianite:** Connecting the Heart and Solar Plexus Chakras, yellow and yellow-green Vesuvianite, also called Idocrase, bridges the gap between the yearnings of emotion and the discipline of the will. If the heart goes one way and the head goes the other, Vesuvianite helps bring them together.

• **Vivianite:** Connecting to the Third Eye Chakra, bluish Vivianite provides perseverance and determination towards achieving spiritual goals. It's a valuable resource during mediation.

• **Wavellite:** When making difficult decisions, aqua-green Wavellite helps provide perspective and clarity. It's also useful in past-life work.

• **Winchite:** Resonating with the Third Eye, silvery-grey Winchite, "The Stone of Tolerance," promotes clairvoyance, intuition and psychic vision.

• **Wolframite:** A stern-feeling stone, reddish-grey Wolframite resonates with the Root Chakra, and imposes order and discipline into your life.

• **Xenotime:** Silvery, fragile Xenotime assists letting go of unwanted people and situations. Carrying a piece can improve focus and energize creativity.

• **Yellow Scapolite:** Resonating with the Sacral Chakra, this honey-yellow gemstone helps manifest prosperity and abundance.

• **Yellow Smithsonite:** Because it resonates with the Sacral Chakra, Yellow Smithsonite is useful for sexual dysfunction, to enhance creativity, and to provide confidence around unfamiliar people and situations.

• **Zebra Stones:** Connecting to the Root Chakra, both black and white Zebra Jasper and Zebra Marble foster creativity and encourage self-expression.

• **Zircon:** Tethering the other Chakras to the Earth Chakra, clear Zircon fosters awareness of one's true spiritual nature. Brownish-red Zircon is known as Jacinth and reddish-orange Zircon is called Hyacinth. All three varieties are associated with the astrological sign of Aquarius.

For more comprehensive lists of stones and crystals, see:
**Encyclopedia of Crystal, Gem, and Metal Magic, Scott Cunningham**
**The Crystal Bible, Judy Hall**
**The Book of Stones, Robert Simmons and Naisha Ahsian**
**Healing Crystals: A-Z Guide to 430 Gemstones, Michæl Gienger**

# CHAPTER FOUR
# AN INTRODUCTION TO NEW THOUGHT

New Thought is a spiritual movement that started in the 19th century. It was founded by the American inventor, mesmerist, and healer Phineas Parkhurst Quimby (1802 - 1866) under the name Mental Science.

Quimby believed that all ailments, mental as well as physical, had their origins in the mind, and *"... if your mind had been deceived by some invisible enemy into a belief, you have put it into the form of a disease, with or without your knowledge. By my theory or truth, I come in contact with your enemy, and restore you to health and happiness. This I do partly mentally, and partly by talking till I correct the wrong impression and establish the Truth, and the Truth is the cure."*

The Mind-Cure approach pioneered by Quimby consisted of him reasoning with his patients until they arrived at the Truth, a healthier state of mind, which he defined as an acceptance of reality, free from wishful thinking and delusions. He reported many cures and success stories.

Quimby's students and 20th century followers drew further ideas about Truth from among the world's great philosophies, including Protestant Christianity, Hinduism, Buddhism, Spiritualism, Subjective Idealism, Transcendentalism; the science of evolution, and practical materialism.

Generally described as a theist, Quimby was not a church-goer, but his teachings led to the founding of religious New Thought denominations such as Christian Science, Religious Science, Unity, Church of Divine Science, Home of Truth, and Missionary Independent Spiritual Church. At the same time, his writings also inspired many secular (non-religious) and metaphysical (occult) practitioners of New Thought.

Because of its wide-ranging origins, the boundaries between religious, secular, and metaphysical New Thought are fluid and permeable. If you wish to distinguish one from the others, it helps to know that religious New Thought practitioners have augmented Quimby's Mind-Cure and Truth with the concept of Affirmative Prayer, while secular New Thought practitioners emphasize the self-help concept of Will, and metaphysical New Thought thinkers additionally bring into play the magical concept of Influence.

Read more about the history of the New Thought Movement online at **ReadersAndRootworkers.org/wiki/Category:Working_Within_ the_New_Thought_Tradition**

## PRINCIPLE BELIEFS OF THE NEW THOUGHT MOVEMENT

New Thought is such an inclusive movement that not all adherents agree on a set of "official" tenets, but many share at least some of these core beliefs:

- There is an infinite, omnipotent, and omnipresent Consciousness.
- Spirit, also called God, is the ultimate, changeless, eternal reality.
- True human nature is divine.
- We create our life experiences through our way of thinking.
- Divinely attuned thought is the ultimate force for good.
- The normal state of life is health; right thinking has a healing effect.
- The goal of life is complete emancipation from all discord.
- Knowledge of these principles is not enough; we must live them.

## THE LAW OF ATTRACTION

If you're familiar with the Law of Attraction, then you understand one of the underlying premises of New Thought. However, most proponents of the Law of Attraction don't seem to fully understand the true power of Mind, which is that mental states can change reality. Most Law of Attraction gurus seem to teach wish-fulfillment: wish for something, and it will happen.

Wishing is a passive activity. There's no real conviction behind it. This is why most people only get small or non-existent returns for their efforts. Mechanically reciting affirmations and desires brings about limited rewards. Most of the motivational trainers and coaches I've known of have only scratched the surface of the potential power available through proper practice of mental induction.

In a nutshell, the fundamental principle is simple:

*Mental states manifest in daily life. Thoughts become real.*

In practice, it's a bit more complicated.

To begin with, this isn't a metaphor. When you successfully change your mental programming, reality will literally change around you. Your luck improves. Prosperity increases. You attract better friends and lovers. People who didn't notice you before suddenly treat you with respect. Your boss suddenly notices you. You make better decisions. You're no longer a victim of fate—you are the master of fate.

## SILENT INFLUENCE

You can go far beyond simply attracting good things into your life. You'll find you can influence the thoughts and actions of other people, change circumstances and conditions, and affect the outcome of events. This is known as "Silent Influence," and it isn't a myth, there's nothing supernatural about it, and many very powerful people practice it today.

If you don't believe that Silent Influence exists, if you don't accept the possibility that the mental influence of one person can change reality, I suggest you take a closer look at history. Some names you might want to pay particular attention to are Alexander the Great, Gandhi, Martin Luther King, Napoleon, the Buddha, Jesus Christ, Adolf Hitler.

Silent Influence isn't a hidden secret. Successful politicians use it. The most charismatic and persuasive speakers and spiritual leaders possess the power. Many people quietly call upon it to get what they want in the world. Silent Influence is the skill Mr. Conlin identified in his writings as the foremost secret to success. We'll take a closer look at this technique later.

## INTENTION AND PREPARATION

The New Thought author Napoleon Hill (1883-1970) suggests in *The Law of Success* that the "secret" of success is the Golden Rule. Only by helping others will we be successful. He also points out that if the desire for prosperity builds in us until it's a burning obsession, then we'll invariably make money. In this seeming paradox lies a great lesson. We have to practice as if we're on fire. But we also have to practice with compassion. Gaining success at the expense of others is a bitter and lonely victory. It's also a tower built on sand. Take another look at history, at the many mighty conquerors who rose to victory, only to plummet in despair at the end. Cæsar had Brutus; Napoleon had his Waterloo, Hitler his bunker in Berlin. Intention is everything, so make sure your intentions are wholesome!

Intention prepares you for either success or failure. The New Thought author Florence Scovel Shinn (1871-1940) wrote, *"The Law of Preparation works both ways. If you prepare for what you fear or don't want, you will begin to attract it. We hear people say, 'I must put away money in case of illness.' They are deliberately preparing to be ill. Or, 'I'm saving for a rainy day,' the rain will surely come, and at an inconvenient time."*

# THE POWER OF THE WORD

The spoken word carries tremendous power. One of the greatest lies you've ever been told is that "Sticks and stones may break my bones, but words will never hurt me." Broken bones heal, and the pain is soon forgotten. But the damage of hurtful words spoken in anger linger for years. Sometimes for a lifetime.

A constant flow of negative, angry, depressed dialogue obsessed with failure, loneliness, and disaster will find manifestation in our immediate environment. Likewise hopeful speech makes for a positive environment. Furthermore, what we say affects everyone with whom we come into contact.

The power of Word isn't limited to verbal speech. Mental dialogue has a subtle influence all its own. If you're lonely and desperate for companionship, you'll manifest desperation, and that's what you'll attract. If you want to manifest loving romance, that's what you have to send out. I've heard so many people say, "I'll never find true love," and guess what? They're right. At least until they change their dialogues. The same applies to "poverty thinking." If all a person dwells upon is the terrible economic forecasts, and how he or she will never get ahead, then these conditions will manifest.

The word made manifest is a very old principle in magical thought. Spell casters know that incantations, blessings, and curses set powerful spiritual vibrations into motion. New Thought practitioners call this "Speaking the Word," and place enormous importance in it. Speaking the Word carries power, and the more spiritually advanced you are, the more authority your word carries. This is why bestowing blessings — and flinging curses — are magical practices found in every culture.

## THE POWER OF PRAYER

Affirmative prayer anticipates a positive outcome rather than a negative one. Instead of complaining to God about your poverty, loneliness, or disease, use affirmative prayer to validate, before God, your ability to work, meet friends, and restore health. In New Thought churches, recitation of Psalms often accompanies affirmative prayer.

For more information on prayers and affirmations, see these books:

**Hoodoo Bible Magic by Miss Michæle and Prof. C. D. Porterfield**
**The Art of Hoodoo Candle Magic by Catherine Yronwode**

## BE CAREFUL WHAT YOU ASK FOR

Just because you want something doesn't mean you'll get it. Let me rephrase that. Just because you want something doesn't mean it's yours.

New Thought teaches that the Universal Mind or Divine Will has set aside somewhere a whole bunch of goodies just for you. All you have to do is claim them. Here's the catch: you have to know how to ask.

I think of it this way: There are things in this world that belong to us or with us, and things that do not. This includes people as well as objects. Often we find ourselves in possession of things or in the company of people that belong to or with someone else, and this creates conflict. Sometimes other people have things or are with people that belong to or with us, and we desperately yearn for them. Much of my work as a spiritual counselor involves helping people figure out which things or people don't belong to or with them. I advise them how to stop clinging to this clutter and let it go, to make room for the things and people that do belong to or with them.

When you pray or attract new experiences into your life, it's important to do it in a way that allows Divine Will room to manifest. For example, you may be infatuated with your good-looking neighbour, and commence a candle ritual to attract him or her into your life. But what if your neighbour doesn't belong with you? This could seriously compromise your spellwork, and even if it's successful, the relationship is going to have problems because you do not belong with one another. It might be wise to perform a divination first.

Everyone knows couples who were "meant for each other." You know who you want, and the Divine Will knows who's yours. So a good request would be: *"My love, I'm seeking you just as you're seeking me. Our two hearts are one. Let's not be apart any longer. Come to me, love. Find me."*

Suppose you have your heart set on a specific house, and you pray to get it. If it is sold to someone else, or you can't afford it, you're heartbroken and you might lose faith in prayer. But the problem wasn't with your prayer skills; it was that you were too specific. Remember that the Divine Will has set aside for you everything you need and the means to obtain it. Rather than trying to manifest a specific house, encode your request for the house that belongs to you. *"I shall obtain the house that's rightfully mine by Universal Law. It's there, waiting for me, as I am searching for it. I am ready to claim it."*

There's a saying that goes, "You can't have everything." Sure you can. All you have to do is ask.

## BE CAREFUL HOW YOU ASK

Allow me to explain proper prayer phraseology with two "bad" examples:

A client requested a vigil light service for "Jerry" to return, but was afraid to use her real name, so she gave her business address as "No Place Like Home" and her name as "No Place." The resultant petition therefore asked God to *"Make Jerry come back"* to *"No Place."* That's no good.

A client chose the self-pitying name "Rejected" and posted a prayer for employment. It read, *"May I find a job speedily. Rejected."* Sure thing — not!

## THE LAW OF NONRESISTANCE

I've often complained how the Law of Attraction is overemphasized while many other principles or "Laws" from New Thought are swept under the carpet. The Law of Nonresistance is one of these.

I'll give an example. We're often advised by "positive thinking" advocates to eliminate negative people from our lives. But everyone has bad days, and if you become so sensitive to "negative" stimuli that you begin protecting yourself as if your mental purity were an African violet, then at the slightest sign of anger, sorrow, fear, or hostility, out comes your moralistic weed-whacker and, "That's it. So-and-so is out." Before too long, we'll eliminate everyone we know from our lives.

The Law of Nonresistance advises that in dealing with confrontational or uncomfortable people, we avoid creating resistance between our way of thinking and theirs. Resistance creates conflict and stress. It's this conflict that drains us of energy, not some imaginary "negative force" radiating from the other person. If someone is suffering, then apply the Golden Rule. Express compassion. Shutting them out is mean and selfish. Our work is fueled by the full force of spiritually focussed desire. I have to question the strength of a person's resolve if it can be turned aside by a brief encounter with a depressed or angry person. The Law of Nonresistance says "go with the flow." This idea is expressed beautifully in Lao Tzu's *Tao Te Ching:*

*Green plants are tender and filled with sap.*
*At their death they are withered and dry.*
*Therefore the stiff and unbending is the disciple of death.*
*The gentle and yielding is the disciple of life.*

## THE LAW OF ACCOUNTABILITY OR KARMA

New Thought incorporates the Biblical injunction "As ye reap, so shall ye sow" in its philosophy. In other words, actions have consequences. This could be called the Law of Accountability. The idea is that if you perform generous deeds and think noble thoughts, good things will return to you. Conversely, mean, spiteful, dishonest, or selfish actions and thoughts bear bitter fruit. If you want to be loved, love. If you want trust, trust others. If you want respect, show respect to others. If you want wealth, perform acts of generosity.

## THE LAW OF CORRESPONDENCE

For every thought the mind can conceive, there is a corresponding external reality, therefore thought, and the external correspondence of that thought, have a mutually-attractive force which work to bring the two together.

To put it simply, if you dwell on disaster in your mind, you'll be drawn toward disaster in reality, and disaster and misfortune will befall you. People sometimes say, "Bad luck just seems to find me." This isn't necessarily just a figure of speech. It could be that we intuitively recognize our own role in the volatile nature of our lives. On the other hand, if you dwell on success and luck, you'll be drawn toward fortunate situations, and success will likewise be drawn toward you.

It isn't necessary to police our every thought. Fleeting, transient notions have a negligible effect on reality. But when the mind dwells continually on a single thought, whether it be health, success, justice, disease, or sorrow, we're naturally drawn toward the external objects of those thoughts. This happens unconsciously, so when incredibly good or bad events manifest, we're often blind to the cause-and-effect correspondence between our internal and external realities, and attribute these inexplicable events to fate, providence, fortune, or magic, unaware of the power we have over our own destinies.

Thoughts, like people, attract and associate with those of similar character. If you send out thoughts of success, prosperity, and charisma, your thoughts will link up with and coalesce with the similar thoughts of others, creating a network of attraction that will draw you together with colleagues and supporters. Likewise, your own negative thoughts of poverty, injustice, and dejection will coalesce in time with those of others and create a dismal quicksand that sucks you into the company of similarly negative thinkers.

# THE POWER OF SILENCE

In Mr. Conlin's writings, as in all New Thought literature, the idea of going into the Silence is often mentioned. This is an important idea of New Thought, and so fundamental to Mr. Conlin's Four Branches of Crystal Gazing that we should go further into it.

Going into the Silence isn't a passive state of not-thinking. You can achieve a blank state by sitting quietly while listening to relaxing music. Going into the Silence, on the other hand, involves cultivating an active state of silent awareness.

Going into the Silence is not making the mind empty, but rather silently contemplating a specific mental or spiritual quality with either Receptive or Projective intent. In the Silence, you can be consciously Receptive, mentally passive, or actively Project a spiritual or material quality such as goodness, compassion, love, or prosperity, either toward a specific individual or toward everything and all beings in general.

There is a difference between meditating on some specific wholesome quality and going into the Silence. During meditation the mind is usually focussed on an object of meditation, even if this object is the mind itself. During meditation, one observes mental states without commentary or judgement. Mental states come and go, and we just watch them, like watching people walking by at the bus stop.

Going into the Silence is similar to meditation, except that rather than contemplating an object of meditation, you enter a place of pure Causation, either Receptive or Projective, and make it your reality. You dwell there, in a creative state, at cause.

If you're focusing on love, you dwell in the Spiritual Realm of Love. If prosperity is your focus, you dwell in the Spiritual Realm of Prosperity. You think, feel, and act as if you have already achieved the object of your desire, and you Project this quality toward your target. If your target is yourself, you attract what you desire to yourself.

What you bring into the Silence is what you send out in Projection work, and what is sent out ultimately manifests in the Realm of Material Reality. We should all take this seriously.

Let me give an example of why the experience of the Silence is so important by taking another look at the differences between meditation and going into the Silence:

Sometimes our minds are filled with unpleasant, disturbing feelings. For instance, when we're not currently involved in a romantic relationship (or unfortunately, sometimes even when we are) we may feel lonely, sad, depressed, anxious, frustrated, and bored. If we don't have enough money to make ends meet, we may feel anxious and panicky. These disturbing feelings can be dealt with by bringing them into meditation. In meditation these feelings become objects of non-judgemental scrutiny. We can either obsess over these feelings or see them as temporary mental states over which we can exercise control. Once we realize we have control over our feelings, they no longer control us, which is a better frame of mind to make wise decisions. This is how meditation can be very useful for controlling disturbing emotions.

Going into the Silence isn't meditation, although you can go into the Silence directly from, or after, a meditation session. Going into the Silence is a base from which to launch Projections and to passively Receive energies. It's a silent dwelling in the Spiritual Realm of your desire.

What you Project, you will surely Receive. This is the true Law of Attraction. What happens in the Silence of your mind plants the seeds that sprout the flowers — or weeds — in your reality. If you bring joy into the Silence, then joy will come to you. If you bring anxiety and loneliness into the Silence, then anxiety and loneliness is what you'll Project, and what you Project will inevitably come back to you. Don't drag anything into the Silence that you don't want showing up later knocking at your door.

Before going into the Silence, banish all feelings and thoughts of fear or poverty from your mind. Meditation before a session can help. Use simple affirmations to create a mindstate of love, confidence, prosperity, and social justice, and then feel this to be true. Make it your reality.

I describe this as taking the desired object out of mindspace and bringing it into heartspace. You won't get results by chanting affirmations and staring into a crystal. You have to really believe. Doubt will kill you in this kind of work. An intellectual effort won't sustain the belief necessary for successful Projective work. You have to enter the space of pure spirit and dwell there.

Rather than trying to think your way through to success, bypass all that mental chatter and go straight to the source of pure experience. If you're sending forth love, don't think love. Be love, and radiate it like you're on fire with it. If you're attracting prosperity, don't wish for it. Find the Realm of Infinite Prosperity in yourself, go into it, and use that ferocious power to reach out and draw more of it to you.

Over the course of time our work builds a cumulative effect on reality. Since mental states are expressed in our daily lives, our minds become protected from unhealthy or negative influences. Our luck improves. Prosperity increases. We attract better friends and lovers. Social justice becomes the norm. Reality literally changes around us.

And if this isn't magic, I don't know my wand from my pointed hat.

I know you must be wondering about the moral implications of using Silent Influence to attain your goals. After all, when exercising the power of Silent Influence over another, you're secretly commanding them to obey your will. But remember the Law of Karma. If you Will your employer to treat you as you deserve and give you the raise you've earned, then all is well. If you Will your husband or wife to act in a loving manner as they should, it's proper. If you send out a request to the Universe to give you what's rightfully yours, where's the blame? Wholesome thoughts are beneficial and are readily accepted by the Universal Mind.

But if you Will someone to cheat, lie or steal on your behalf, or to leave their spouse and commit adultery with you, or any other action that you know is wrong, then you will reap what you sow. Your evil deed will come back to you. Evil thoughts are destructive and tear away at the harmonious fabric of reality, and the Universal Mind resists them.

I invite you to look at history, and see for yourself how evil people of great power have paid in bitter coin for their destructive legacies.

## PROJECTING AND RECEIVING

Two cognitive operations practiced by early New Thought adepts were Projection and Reception. Projection is based on the theory that your thoughts can be focussed and sent out to influence people and events, and Reception is the flip side of the coin, based on the theory that your mind attracts and is affected by the fruits of your own and other individuals' Projections.

Mr. Conlin taught members of the Crystal Silence League how to do both Projection and Reception with the assistance of crystal balls. It was a stroke of pure genius that he realized that these exercises could be magnified and focussed with a crystal. We'll take a closer look at Projection and Reception in Chapter Five, on The Four Branches of Crystal Gazing and look at a great way to enhance Attraction work in Chapter Seven, on Chakra-Enhanced Crystal Work.

## THE INFLUENCE OF BUDDHISM AND HINDUISM

During the 19th century great interest in Asian philosophy melded with the growth of a widespread metaphysical revival. Spiritual and occult authors became quite interested in Buddhism and Oriental esoteric knowledge. The American occultist Paschal Beverley Randolph had travelled to India to study magic as early as 1850, and his British friend, the Reverend Hargrave Jennings, published a famous book titled *The Indian Religions or, Results of the Mysterious Buddhism.* Helena Petrovna Blavatsky and Henry Steel Olcott of the Theosophical Society brought Theravada Buddhism to New York around 1875, and in 1893, the Parliament of the World's Religions was held in Chicago, and America got its first close-up look at an authentic Hindu yogi, Swami Vivekananda.

I often wonder if Mr. Conlin studied with a guru during his many travels. In his writings, he mentions "Hindu" techniques, indicating a familiarity with yogic practice. He also refers to a "Swami Panchadasi," but this was simply one of many pseudonyms of his friend, the occult author William Walker Atkinson. Whether his knowledge arose from personal instruction or the study of recently-translated manuscripts, such as the *Bardo Thodol (Tibetan Book of the Dead)* I can't say, but another ancient Asian text of particular interest to those who seek out Conlin's sources is the 1st century *Epitome of the Great Symbol*, which teaches an ancient yogic meditation technique aimed at achieving Nirvana. In this book we find:

*(12) The observing of silence, after the casting out the dead breath of exhalation, is called the tranquility or immobility of speech ...*
*(27) Meditate upon thy guru as being seated upon the Crown of thy head ... and pray to him, 'Vouchsafe to me Thy gift-waves, that I may obtain the highest boon of the Great Symbol.'*
*(28) Then having prayed for the boon-conferring 'gift-waves,' absorb them into thyself. Think that thy mind is blended with the Divine Mind.*

The commentator goes on to explain that these 'gift-waves' are psychic energies sent out via telepathic transmission by gurus.

You can't help noticing the similarities to Conlin's descriptions of Projection and Reception in the Silence!

In *The Secret of Concentration* (1924) Mr. Conlin relates an anecdote told to him by a young man whose father was stationed in Benares, India. A group of yogis prepared for a demonstration of their mystical powers by meditating for hours each day, staring at small, bright crystals on the ground. After several days of meditation, they gathered a crowd and performed incredible feats of wizardry. Among these feats was the famous Indian Rope Trick, where a rope thrown into the air remained suspended by nothing but the willpower of the yogi. With the rope dangling in mid-air, a small boy climbed to the top and disappeared!

Skeptics have dismissed the Indian Rope Trick as a legend or a performance of legerdemain. But Mr. Conlin's anecdote provides a clue to another explanation. When the young man examined photographs he had made of the unbelievable feat, the photos showed only a crowd of people standing around the group of yogis, staring upward. There was neither rope nor boy. The yogis had apparently implanted the images in everyone's minds through mental Projection.

The man's father explained the secret was to concentrate your mind on one thought to the exclusion of everything else, and that's what the yogis had been doing by staring for hours at the bits of shiny crystal. From this experience the man gleaned the power of Silent Influence, which he mastered to a remarkable degree and utilized several times in his own life.

## THE INFLUENCE OF CHRISTIANITY AND SPIRITUALISM

The 19th and 20th century developers of religious, secular, and metaphysical New Thought were primarily raised in Christian churches. Their early training and beliefs contributed to the form that New Thought subsequently took. The denominations that contributed the most members to New Thought were Protestant, including the Methodists, Presbyterians, Baptists, and Lutherans. To them we owe the many Biblical concepts and quotations found in New Thought teachings

The religion of Spiritualism came into existence around the same time as New Thought. Spiritualist cosmology, which includes communication with the dead, was not part of early New Thought doctrine, but over time, many Spiritualists adopted aspects of New Thought beliefs, and some New Thought teachers, including Mr. Conlin, practiced and advocated Spiritualist mediumship and communion with the dead in a New Thought context.

# CHAPTER FIVE
# THE FOUR BRANCHES OF CRYSTAL GAZING

Mr. Claude Conlin was an extraordinary and enigmatic man. He rose from virtual obscurity in the rural Midwest to become one of the most successful and prosperous people of his time, and counted among his acquaintances and friends the then-prominent Hollywood stars Clara Bow, Marion Davies, Jackie Coogan, Harold Lloyd, and Margaret Sullivan. He married, purchased property, and retired a millionaire after only nine years on the public stage.

Affluence and fame such as that enjoyed by Mr. Conlin doesn't happen by accident. He deliberately set out to succeed at life, and the more he accomplished, the more he wanted others to enjoy life as he did. Even while touring the country as a performer, he had begun to write and publish small booklets in which he shared his philosophy and his methodology. After his retirement, he published books on New Thought and prayed every morning over the postcards of those who sent him prayer requests.

Mr. Conlin was a great master of Silent Influence and all other methods of Projection and Attraction. How pleased and excited he must have been when he discovered that crystal balls could magnify and focus mental waves! With that knowledge, he made the leap from entertainer to teacher.

Proficiency in crystal-work techniques comes at a price. Practice is that price, and lots of it. You have to carefully train your mind and body. Mr. Conlin stresses in all his writings the importance of taking care of yourself and diligently training your mind. He emphasizes a healthy diet, plenty of rest, exercise, avoiding indulgence in alcohol and other intoxicants, a dedication to spiritual excellence, and a program of meditation to hone mental concentration. He often sounds like a stern parent:

> *If you want to sacrifice your mental control and whole future life for a few pleasant indulgences in the present that is your business … if you do not take advantage of its benefits, IT IS BECAUSE YOU DO NOT WANT TO.*

My goodness! If at times Mr. Conlin seemed abrupt, he knew he had a serious message to deliver, and he didn't have time for curious dilettantes. He was out to change the world.

# THE FIRST BRANCH OF CRYSTAL GAZING:
# THE VISIONARY BRANCH:
# SCRYING, CRYSTALLOMANCY, OR SEERSHIP

The First Branch of Mr. Conlin's Crystal Gazing is the Visionary Branch, also called Crystallomancy, Divination, Scrying, or Seership, and it's by far the most difficult. Visionary work involves gazing into a crystal, or any shiny or translucent surface, for the purpose of seeing images, which are interpreted for divinatory purposes. Scrying is an advanced mystical art that few ever truly master — but many can become quite proficient with practice.

## A SCRYER'S TOOLS

Crystal balls have been used for centuries as scrying devices. The cliché of the scarf-wrapped seer peering intently into his or her glowing orb is promoted in the media and parodied in advertisements and comedy skits. Just because crystal balls are used as props in bad movies is no reason to scoff at their effectiveness. Tarot cards have also fallen into cliché status, and yet some of the best readers still use them.

A crystal ball isn't essential for scrying. Seers such as Nostradamus saw visions in a bowl of water, and Joseph used a cup for divination. Black ink, mirrors, and shiny stones have also been used. But there's something pure and lovely about the crystal ball that arrests attention, and when Mr. Conlin developed his Four Branches, he chose the sphere. Perhaps did this because when practicing Projection, a crystal orb is omni-directional. It sends mental waves in every direction. You can't do that with a mirror, or a bowl of water.

## PALM STONES AND SHEW-STONES

In addition to reading spherical crystal or glass balls, crystallomancers have also long made use of palm stones. These are flat, smoothly irregular pieces of glossy stone, such as Obsidian, Carnelian, Calcite, or Selenite, that fit into the palm of the hand and are used in divination.

Similar to palm stones are shew-stones of Clear Quartz that have been river-tumbled or roughed up in a machine to create a white surface, then cut across to make a smooth, polished "window" into the interior. Rounder than conventional palm stones, they too are held in the hand for divination.

## THE BEST CRYSTAL POINTS AND STONES FOR GAZING

Mr. Conlin mentions the use of crystal points, stones, and other shiny natural objects by seers of all cultures in the prefatory remarks of *Crystals and Crystal Gazing*. You'll find any scrying technique you master with a crystal ball equally effective with crystal points and stones. While any transparent or shiny medium yields itself to scrying, certain crystals are believed to enhance clairvoyant talents. These are:

| | | | |
|---|---|---|---|
| • Amethyst | • Aquamarine | • Azurite | • Beryl |
| • Carnelian | • Citrine | • Clear Quartz | • Emerald |
| • Flint | • Heliodor | • Hematite | • Jet |
| • Lapis Lazuli | • Moonstone | • Morganite | • Obsidian |
| • Opal | • Sapphire | • Tiger's Eye | • White Calcite |

## GEMSTONE JEWELRY FOR SCRYING

Many stones and crystals are available as roughs, points, tumbles, or spheres, but others — especially the brightly transparent crystal gemstones — are better worn in rings or necklaces for scrying purposes. For one thing, the availability of certain crystals as palm stones, points, or spheres is limited by their mineralogical growth pattern. There are no 2-inch diameter Pyrope Garnet spheres, for instance, because the crystals simply do not grow to that size. Second, in many cases, the cost is too high; few individuals will be able to afford a substantial table-size Amethyst sphere, even if it did come on the market. Third, crystals are heavy, and if you are a traveller, a small scrying stone — especially one that looks like jewelry and can unobtrusively double as a protective charm or lucky talisman — will serve you very well.

Since ancient times, small gemstones set in silver, gold, or a combination of the two, have filled the need for portable scrying tools.

One way to wear such a scrying stone is to have it set in a ring. Depending on the stone, it can be a smoothly domed cabochon or a sparkling faceted gem. Scrying stones of the Beryl family, all quite costly in the larger sizes, are well within the range of most people when worn as rings. A necklace pendant in an open setting makes a great portable scrying stone too, and it can double as a divinatory pendulum. Or you can simply wear it to match your scrying ring, and folks will comment favourably on your fashion sense.

## FROM ROCK CRYSTAL TO FUSED QUARTZ

A large crystal ball, if mined of Rock Quartz, free from all imperfections and internal fractures, would be too expensive for most workers to own. Figured, translucent, chatoyant, and opaque spheres of polished Agate, Rose Quartz. Calcite, Obsidian, Tiger's Eye, Jasper, Fuchsite, or Selenite make fine scrying stones at reasonable prices. The famous root worker Dr. Jim Jordon of Como, North Carolina, for instance, was known far and wide during the 1920s through the 1960s for his use of a figured stone palm ball, not a clear crystal ball. But if you wish to own a very large Clear Quartz ball, then Fused Quartz — crushed Quartz stone that has been melted in a furnace to create a uniform texture — is a reasonably priced alternative to natural Quartz. Fine glass spheres make excellent gazing balls too.

## COLOURED GLASS CRYSTAL BALLS

Just as certain natural crystals and stones lend themselves to specific conditions, so do tinted crystal glass balls.

In his book, *Personal Lessons, Codes, and Instructions for Members of the Crystal Silence League,* Mr. Conlin suggests the use of coloured glass crystal balls when sending out or attracting certain conditions.

- **Clear Crystal:** The universal sender and receiver, useful in all aspects of crystal ball work.
- **Aqua or Blue Crystal:** Employed in health, tranquility, spirituality, and preace work. Good for reception but not very powerful for Projection.
- **Red Crystal:** Employed for love, sexuality, action, adventure, blood. It takes a great deal of passion to send with a red crystal, but as a receiver, red is a strengthener of the physical and spiritual heart.
- **Green Crystal:** Used for prosperity, money, and business. It takes someone with a generous heart to be a good sender with green crystals.
- **Yellow, Honey-Amber, or Purple Crystal:** Employed to work with success, career, personal power, travel, and legal matters. These are good for sending and receiving.
- **Black Crystal:** Employed to absorb negativity and evil spirits. Mr. Conlin says Black is the "ultimate receiver," and as a sender it requires "Masterful Will."

## CHOOSING THE SIZE OF YOUR CRYSTAL BALL

Beginners to crystal ball work are often surprised at the wide range of sizes presented when shopping for their first crystal ball. It's easy to get carried away and buy a huge, bowling-ball sized crystal — but before you do, take into consideration some practical concerns.

You'll want to hold your crystal to charge it and become familiar with it. Many visualization exercises also require you to hold the ball for several minutes at a sitting. Even holding a crystal the size of a baseball can quickly grow tiring, and larger crystals are more likely to crack if you drop them. Since the larger crystals are expensive, this can be heartbreaking.

While it's very cool to have all these large crystal balls decorating your occult parlour, in a practical sense a smaller ball is better. It takes a great deal of spiritual power to work with larger crystals.

I advise beginners to commence their exercises with a two-inch clear crystal ball. When you gain proficiency, work up to a three-inch palm ball and tinted crystals. If you have small hands and like the palm method of holding the ball, a two-and-a-half-inch ball may be the best size for you.

For my Projections for the Crystal Silence League, when I'm launching a powerful Projection of enormous scope, I use a four-inch ball, but I've been doing this for a long time. The crystal ball used for Crystal Silence League Projections at Missionary Independent Spiritual Church is a massive ten-inch clear sphere of Fused Quartz.

## HOW TO POSITION YOUR CRYSTAL BALL

Several positions are used for scrying with a sphere. Try them all — then select a combination of sphere size and physical comfort that's right for you:

**1. Finger Position:** Hold a very small ball between thumb and fingers, near the eyes. Brace your elbow on a table or chair arm and gaze into the ball.
**2. Palm Position:** Hold a small ball is in the palm of one hand. Brace your elbow on a table, chair arm, or your hip bone and gaze into the ball.
**3. Double Handed:** Rest a mid-size ball in both your hands, using them as a stand. Brace your elbows on the table and gaze into the ball.
**3. Lap Position:** Rest a mid-size ball in your lap and gaze down into it.
**4. Table Position:** Place a large ball in a stand on a table, below eye level.

## PREPARATION FOR SCRYING

Traditionally, spheres are considered the best solid for scrying, and orbs intended for scrying purposes are cleansed by moonlight. Take your ball outside, hold it up to the moon (the full moon is best, but not essential) and send all your positive energy into the ball. Over time you develop an affinity for your crystal, just as you do for most of your tools. The more you work with a particular tool, the more you feel its potential. I'm reluctant to suggest that you can bond with an inanimate object such as crystals and stones, but sometimes you do begin to feel a sense of affection for tools that serve you well. The more you work with crystal balls the more you come to love them.

Wrap the ball in cloth, or put it in a bag and it's ready.

Mr. Conlin suggests several introductory exercises in Crystal Gazing. Hold your crystal while fixing your undivided attention on it for five minutes (he notes that this is hard to do in the beginning). Alternatively, place the ball on a shelf at eye level, aiming your forefinger at it, and as you walk toward the ball, keep your finger in alignment with the ball. Concentrate on the tip of your finger—and the ball—until you touch the ball.

In addition to his suggestions, the following exercises help develop concentration skills while developing your ability to see images in a crystal.

## FLAME GAZING WITH A CRYSTAL

I learned this method as a teenager, and I still practice it quite often.

Sit in a dark room and place a candle on a table or on the floor if that's where you're sitting, and hold the crystal ball so you're watching the flickering flame through the ball. Relax, take three deep breaths, and gaze into the ball. Let your eyes move in and out of focus as you see various images rise and fall in the ball. The trick is to look through the ball without letting your eyes focus on anything in particular. You can roll and rotate the ball if you like.

Allow your mind to free-associate with these images. Don't try to force meaning on the images, or link them together in a meaningful pattern. You'll find that after a while, without trying, you'll unconsciously start to construct a narrative. If you've never experienced this mental phenomenon before, prepare for a shock because it's quite startling the first time it happens. It's as if the ball is telling you a story.

## SKY GAZING WITH A CRYSTAL

This lovely method was shown to me by a Sioux shaman, who did it with a Quartz point. I brought out my small crystal ball and asked him to teach the technique to me. He was intrigued by the idea of using a clear ball and we exchanged crystals, mine for his, and took turns gazing through them for several hours. I loved the new experience of gazing through Rutilated Quartz, and soon obtained a piece of my own for gazing.

This method is exactly what it says. You go outside on a partly cloudy day and watch the clouds through your crystal ball. Relax your mind, allowing your intuitive processes free rein. You can do this any time, day or night, and I especially urge you to gaze at the stars and moon.

Gaze at a rainbow if you get the opportunity. I once gazed at a moonbow, and experienced fantastic visions. If you don't know what a moonbow is, this is a rainbow created near a waterfall at night by a full moon. This convergence of events manifests tremendous spiritual opportunities if you watch for them.

Never gaze directly at the sun or at the sky if the sunlight is bright. You can blind yourself that way.

## WATER GAZING WITH A CRYSTAL

While water itself has been used as a scrying material since ancient times, gazing at moving water through your crystal ball has a mesmerizing effect that can facilitate trance. Appreciate the sound of the rippling water in Nature as you gaze through the ball. Try this method if you find yourself experiencing difficulty "letting go" of conscious control of your thoughts, or relaxing from the tensions and stresses of the day.

## BEGINNING TO SEE IMAGES

Seeing images does not come easily to all students. Sometimes it helps if you focus your mind on a question, topic or person before gazing. Other times you'll approach the crystal with no expectations just to see what it will say to you. Once you begin seeing images and creating narratives from your visions, you can check these visions against your daily experiences to correlate their meanings. It helps to keep a journal.

## WHAT DO THESE IMAGES MEAN?

Sometimes the meanings of images are clear. If you see a dog, and your daughter brings home a puppy, that's fairly straightforward. However, if you see two birds, a book, and a stone tower, you might need to interpret the signs. Lenormand card readers would know what to make of it; others might have to consult an interpreter.

A knowledge of symbols and their meanings helps, but in my experience, scryers almost always see images that make personal sense to them. Many instruction manuals provide long lists of symbols. You can study theories of universal archetypes, or buy a book on tea leaf readers' symbols, but over time you'll build your own vocabulary of images. I call this your Personal Iconography—your personal set of sacred symbols.

## ADVANCED SCRYING: MEDIUMSHIP

Contacting the Spirit Realm is a fascinating and delicate matter. It also requires confidence and cultivation. The first question you should ask is whether or not you have a gift for mediumship. Not everyone does. If you don't, you can still develop mediumship skills, but it will require study.

If you have a gift for spirit communication, you probably already know it and the question is moot. How do you know? Spirits tend to manifest to those who can see or hear them, and natural mediums often begin seeing spirits at a very young age.

My first experience with spirit visitation occurred when I was four years old. I was having trouble falling asleep due to a stomach ache. My grandfather came in, sat on the bed next to me, and rubbed my belly and sang to me until I drifted into sleep. When I told my mom and aunt at breakfast about my grandfather's nighttime visit, they exchanged a troubled glance. My mom told me I must have dreamed the episode, because my grandfather had died during the night. I didn't understand the meaning of this until his funeral, when I realized that his ghost must have come to say goodbye to me.

That night time appearance by my grandfather was my first experience with the idea that there is a part of us that survives the death of the body, and that this part — this spirit — can still care about and interact with the living. What this spiritual part of us is, I do not know, nor does anyone, in my opinion, but it exists, and some people can sense its existence.

If you're not a natural medium, don't despair. The knack can be developed, although it isn't easy. Sometimes it's best to start with more solid materials before trying to work with the ethereal planes. Mediumship can also take another form, that of telepathic communication with other, living, people. Through clairvoyant means, you can sense another person's mind and glean insights into that person's life.

This isn't, in the strictest sense, mind-reading. You usually can't ask someone to think of a number from 1-100, look into your crystal ball, and guess the number — although I've attended intense crystal ball sessions where the participants succeeded in tests similar to this. Someone visualized an object, and the other participants gazed into their crystals and tried to guess the thought. In some of these sessions, the success rate was startling.

Telepathic communication through crystal gazing is not usually direct, but is more of a feeling, mental impression, or sense of knowing.

Start by concentrating on a specific person in the next room or several miles away, and picture this person vividly in your mind. Gazing into your crystal, Project your concentration outward, searching for this person. At some point, you might feel a strong sense of contact with the person. Concentrating further, you might sense this person's emotional state, you will learn if their feelings toward you are honest or unreliable, if they can be trusted or not, if the person safe or in danger. If you refine this ability to its highest point of sensitivity, you might even be able to see through their eyes.

How does this help you connect to spirits? The strange and wonderful aspect of this technique is that it isn't limited to living beings.

Mind or consciousness is a mysterious process, not fully understood, and it seems simplistic to assume that consciousness arises solely from the inert matter of the brain. Survival of consciousness after the death of the body doesn't prevent communication between the living and the dead. It just introduces complications. So once you've developed the knack of connecting mind-to-mind with another person, try connecting with the spirit of a loved one who has passed on to the Spirit Realm.

It may help at first to use a photo for focus. Concentrate on the picture and imagine the person as they were in life. Try to recall their smell, sound of their voice, and their laugh. Now, just as you did with the living person, Project your mind out and search for them. Don't be discouraged if your first attempts don't succeed. Spirits exist on a much more subtle plane than we, and it may require practice to learn to "tune in" on the proper frequency.

# THE SECOND BRANCH OF CRYSTAL GAZING:
## THE PROJECTIVE BRANCH:
### SILENT INFLUENCE OR SENDING

Indirectly influencing the actions of others from a distance is an awesome and powerful proposition, and one on which Mr. Conlin placed a great deal of emphasis. As he points out, every spell cast, every prayer chanted, every wish made, are attempts to influence the will or thoughts of someone else.Through the eye of the crystal ball, your will is focussed, concentrated and hurled out toward the object of your desire. As Mr. Conlin put it, "By use of the Crystal, you may Project or broadcast messages of Psychic Influence to those whom you have never met, and your prayers for them will change and influence their lives."

What does this mean? It means that if you have an important business meeting, you might send out thoughts of Silent Influence before you meet your clients, urging them to see you in a favourable light. It means that if you're appearing in court, you might attempt to sway the judge in your favour through your crystal ball several days before your hearing.

Silent Influence isn't limited to people. You can penetrate the very fabric of reality if you're determined, and reweave it to your preferences. You can attract love, prosperity, success, fortune, fame.

These techniques work. Mr. Conlin became the highest paid stage performer of his time. He was a contemporary of the famous escape artist Harry Houdini, and when the two appeared on the same bill Mr. Conlin (performing under the name "Alexander, the Man Who Knows") was paid a higher fee, and his name was larger on the theater posters.

To initiate a Projection, your mind must be absolutely clear before going into the Silence. Put aside anything distracting. You can't harbour thoughts of anger or anxiety. Be calm, confident, assured, and focussed. Banish any feelings of uncertainty. Doubt will kill your success in this kind of work.

Proficiency in meditation helps develop the sort of focus and concentration you need to make significant progress with Silent Influence. Think of narrowing the focus of your attention to a laser beam which you're going to fire into the heart of your crystal ball.

You can hold the crystal in your hand or rest it on a stand, and if you're using complimentary crystals (see Chapter Six) for your stand, select crystals appropriate to the condition which you're empowering.

Visualize your target, and the more sensory detail you engage the better. Try to see, hear, smell them if possible, and touch them. Imagine your target performing the actions you wish of them. Talk to the mental version of your target through it: *"Mr. Jones, you know I'm the best employee you have. You will recognize this. You DO recognize this and wish to reward me. You're offering me a raise and a promotion. And I'm grateful, and I accept."*

When you've fueled this scenario with every ounce of the fire of your convictions, hurl it into the crystal and then outward to your target (in this case the hypothetical Mr. Jones). And then let it go. Relax.

## CODES: THE SECRET MESSAGES OF THE SOUL

Silent Influence can be initiated for specific situations, such as getting a raise, or for general matters, like prosperity, with no target in mind. When a situation is ongoing or long-term, it helps to Project with brief "Codes."

Codes are what Mr. Conlin called extremely short, pithy statements affirming the intention of a desire. He suggested that we keep them as condensed as possible. He called these abbreviated affirmations Codes because he believed they were encrypted messages which, when expanded in the mind of the Receiver, initiated important transformations.

Here is an example of Mr. Conlin's Code for Friendship: *"I am happy in the confidence of my friend, (person's name). We are agreed. We are in harmony. We are united. My friend is drawing nearer to me daily."*

Like lengthier affirmations, Codes are always positive. Instead of "I will stop snacking between meals," try a brief, empowering Code like *"I'm happy to feel hunger, for I am strong and brave and I finish my work before eating."*

Compressed Codes are so powerful that I suggest to my clients that when they're sending for an unknown romantic partner they should not give me a list of traits they want in a partner: funny, good provider, loyal, attractive, great in bed, dutiful parent, passionate, artistic, smart — this isn't necessary. All of it can be encoded in your Projection. You know what you want. All unspoken assumptions ride the wave of that desire. All you need to do is clearly feel the person's presence in your heart, and then think clearly your Code: *"Come to me my love. I'm looking for you just as you are looking for me."*

This is the secret of successful Projection. After entering the Silence, you must act and feel as if you've already made the changes which you're trying to initiate. You must believe. The strength of your belief will change reality.

# HARMONIZED CRYSTALS IN PROJECTION WORK

It's well-known that certain coloured crystals are attuned for work in specific areas. Red or pink crystals are best for love work, and green for money work. Here's an idea to boost the power of your Projective Attraction work through the use of harmonized crystals.

By harmonized crystals, I don't necessarily mean crystals of similar colour, although hue may play a role in their selection. I also do not mean stones of similar mineralogical makeup, although that too may be a factor in your choice. Nor do I mean that their forms must be similar — all roughs or all points, for instance, although, again, you may select them according to that criterion if you wish. What i am proposing here is merely' this: select two or more crystals that are similar enough in vibrational harmony that they complement each other.

Try these experiments until you learn how to select harmonized stones: Construct a stand of three crystals on which you will rest a glass crystal ball. Arrange three crystals or stones in a tight circle, and rest the crystal ball on the crystals. What crystals you use, and what coloured crystal ball, will depend on the type of work or spell you're performing. For example:

- **Money:** Iron Pyrite, Jade, Green Aventurine. Arrange together in a ring formation, and place a small (2") green crystal ball on the stones.
- **Love:** Pink Tourmaline, Rose Quartz, Red Jasper. Arrange together in a ring formation and place a small (2") red crystal ball on the stones.
- **Work:** Tiger's Eye, Carnelian, Hematite. Arrange in a ring formation, and place a small (2") honey-amber crystal ball on the stones.
- **Luck:** Amazonite, Garnet, Smoky Quartz. Arrange in a ring formation, and place a small (2") yellow crystal on the stones.

You get the idea. By using three harmonized crystals to support a tinted glass ball, you engorge your Projections with power and magnify their range. But don't stop there. Try four faceted gemstones beneath a clear glass ball, Try a ring of six stones of two alternating varieties.

The possibilities are almost endless, but by using trial and error, you'll soon be able to create your own favourite sets. All you need is a strong psychic intuition, possibly augmented with a crystal encyclopedia and a manual of mineralogy to get you thinking of stones you've never met before.

## TIGER'S EYE PROJECTION AND PRAYER EXERCISE

If this is your first exposure to Projective techniques I understand it can be intimidating, so here's a simple exercise with a stone to get you started:

Polished Tiger's Eye is associated with wealth and personal protection, excellent areas of focus for mental Projections, or Codes, as Mr. Conlin termed them. This Projection uses Tiger's Eye for career enhancement:

1. Sit comfortably in a quiet room where you won't be interrupted.
2. Hold the Tiger's Eye in your hand.
3. Focus your thoughts on the Tiger's Eye as you take three deep breaths.
4. Go into the Silence.
5. Phrase your Code in the present tense: *"I am prosperous and successful. I have sufficient resources and generosity to meet my needs and help others. I am happy at my ideal job and appreciated in my profession."*
6. If you are Projecting prosperous career prayers for another person, the same idea applies: *"John, hear me now. You are happy, successful, and prosperous. You are well pleased in your ideal profession and admired by your co-workers. You are being promoting rapidly to positions of greater responsibility and increased salary."*

Repeat these affirmations as necessary to achieve your desired result.

## HEALING PROJECTION WITH FOUR STONES

Next, try a simple exercise with four harmonized crystals. This is a Projection for distance healing. The stones are soothing lunar Selenite, gently comforting Rose Quartz, toxin-repelling Amethyst, and negativity-absorbing Black Obsidian. Use either four spheres or four small tumble-polished specimens. Lay a photograph of the person you are assisting on a table and place one stone on each of the four corners of the photograph.

1. Sit comfortably and focus on the photo and stones as you breathe.
2. Go into the Silence.
3. Project your Code: *"Joyfully I see you (person's name) in health, strong, well, restored, active, and happy. You are free of pain, made whole in body and mind."*

## PUNCHING HOLES IN SPACE

This is as good a time as any to bring up the subject of the Astral Tube, a technique Mr. Conlin mentions in *Crystals and Crystal Gazing* which many occult practitioners call upon to help visualize their target.

Envision a tube, about a foot in diameter, between you and your target, through which you can see them. Your end of the tube extends from your crystal ball. You peer through the ball at your target and send your Projections. If working with a three- to four-inch ball, hold it between your cupped hands and peer through it like a lens. If you're using a smaller ball, place it inside your curled index finger and thumb, and hold it to your eye like a telescope.

Mr. Conlin left it at that, but I suggest you go a bit further with the Astral Tube. Once you've established visual contact with your target, widen the Tube into a Tunnel, walk through it, and stand facing your target. Place the ball between you, forehead-to-forehead (connecting your Third Eye with theirs) and Project your Codes directly into their head.

Similar to the Astral Tube is the Silver Cord, another old mind-reader's technique. In this one, you leave your body and travel into astral space, connected to yourself only by a silver cord. Guided by the light of your crystal, you can visit people in their homes, especially while they sleep, and Project mental Codes into their minds. When finished, you reel yourself back in along the Silver Cord until you are once again in your body.

## THE INSIDIOUS HIDDEN SECRET OF MIND-READING

While on the subject of getting into people's heads, there is a secret technique hinted, but never quite overtly described, in Mr. Conlin's writings. This secret is so insidiously subtle, so potentially powerful, that when it dawned on me what he was insinuating (hiding behind circumlocutions, to be discovered like buried treasure by those who very carefully studied his work) I couldn't believe such a thing was possible.

What Mr. Conlin seemed to suggest was pushing a mental Projection far past the point of merely sending a code to your target. Mr. Conlin hints that it's possible to have a mental conversation with them. During this astral conversation, you literally ask your target what is required to obtain the specific goal you desire. You probe their mind for the secret information you need to ensure your success.

I want you to pause for a moment to let that sink in. You want something from someone. This is a way to secretly ask them, without their knowledge, how to get it.

For example, let's say you have a job interview with Mr. Smythe in a couple of days. You're competing with five other, equally qualified people for the position. You've completed your Projection of Mental Influence toward Mr. Smythe to recognize you as the best person for the job. Now continue to push, until you're in direct mind-to-mind contact with him, and ask, *"What will it take to ensure I get this position? What specifically will I need to say or do to convince you I'm the person for this job?"*

Mr. Smythe might answer, *"I'm looking for someone who's not afraid to disagree with me if necessary. I'm surrounded by yes-men. I want a manager who'll challenge my decisions if they have a better idea."*

Armed with this information, you can approach the interview with a winning strategy. In most interviews, you're usually asked to describe your strengths. Knowing Mr. Smythe's mind, you can say, *"Well, I don't know if this is exactly a strength, because not all of my previous employers liked it. But I have a lot of my own ideas, which I tend to express, especially if it's for the good of the company. At times this put me at odds with other managers who just seemed to want to do the same old things over and over."*

If your goal is to win the heart of your true love, but he has issues from a previous relationship that prevent him from opening his heart, send your Projected Codes as usual. *"My love, we're meant to be together, your heart and mine are one."* Then, applying these deeper techniques, go into his mind and invite a conversation. Be very careful. If you feel resistance, back away and try again another time. Don't insist. Forcing yourself into someone's mind is a form of psychic rape and that isn't acceptable under any circumstances.

If your beloved accepts your invitation, embrace him with all your love. Tell him how much you love him and how precious he is to you. Ask him how you can help heal the hurts from the past. Now be quiet and listen, and when I say listen, I mean do so with everything you have. Listen with your heart, and pay attention as if your life depended on it. Your lover, if he truly wants to be closer, will whisper the secrets his heart so desperately wants to tell you, but which he cannot speak out loud.

Mr. Conlin only vaguely hints at this technique, and he never explains how to do it. But if you've mastered Silent Influence you'll find it only takes a little practice to take it to this next level.

# IS THIS RIGHT?

When I've discussed these mind-power techniques with various people over the years questions concerning ethical implications often come up. Is it wrong to use Silent Influence and Silent Interrogation for personal gain? It depends. There's no dishonour in prosperity, just as there's no nobility in poverty. You can't have peace of mind and spiritual contentment while struggling with basic survival. However, greed and lust are not noble, and power hunger leads to bad consequences for everyone. But it's possible to be prosperous while remaining compassionate and generous, have a good job without ruining anyone, and be loved by many without being a narcissistic egomaniac. Remember, the universe is filled with wonderful things, and many of those things belong to you. It's no sin to collect your own winnings.

We strive for jobs, money, space, living quarters, romantic partners. The world is a competitive place. Nature is nothing but an ongoing battleground for survival. When you gaze out on a beautiful, sunny day at the lake, admiring the lovely trees, bushes, and water, this tranquility is an illusion. One inch below all that beauty, everyone is busily killing and eating everyone else. This isn't horrible; it's Nature's beautiful and relentless way.

Mankind, at least currently, is in charge of the earth because we're more cunning and clever than anything else. We were able to outrun, out-climb, or out-think predators that tried to eat us. Call it Divine Providence or evolution, that's how we got here, and we're very good at defending our position.

Silent Influence, along with other psychic skills, is a latent ability we all have. Like all abilities, we can choose to nurture it or leave it lying dormant in the sleeping Realm of Potentiality. Most will never bother, convinced there's no other choice than to live, as Thoreau put it, "lives of quiet desperation." A very small number realize their potential and take control of their situation. Some of these individuals are good-hearted, ethical human beings. Others aren't.

If you're worried about the ethics of using every bit of your power to claim what's already yours, just remember that the Divine Mind has a way of dealing with those who deal unjustly with their fellow beings. The playing field always gets levelled in the long run.

Claim your share, and enjoy it to the fullest. But always keep your fellow beings close to you in your mind and heart, and share with them the fruits of your success.

# THE THIRD BRANCH OF CRYSTAL GAZING:
# THE RECEPTIVE BRANCH:
# INDUCTION OR RECEIVING

Pastors and members of the Crystal Silence League create affirmative Projections, via our crystals, three times a day: morning, afternoon, and night. Anyone can Receive theses "tonics" as Mr. Conlin called them, simply by entering a Receptive state and allowing the waves to flood in.

But in addition to the invigorating affirmations from the League, there is an infinite storehouse of power waiting for you to claim it, and here the power of crystal reception reaches its fullest potential.

Imagine an ocean of pure power whose reserves you could tap to sustain you when you're tired, infuse stamina to your works, bring prosperous attraction to your every decision, endow you with love and success. This power flows from the universe, the collective mind of all conscious beings past and present, and is inexhaustible. By mastering the technique of Induction or Receiving, you can drink all you want from that depthless source.

Some Reception happens automatically. That which is Projected must be Received, and once you've launched a Projection, your mind anticipates Receiving that for which you've asked. When you're sending a Projection, part of your mind is also in a Receptive mode. If you send thoughts of love, for example, those very thoughts become objects of attraction. You'll automatically attract love toward you, as a magnet attracts paper clips.

But what if you didn't send a Projection toward a person or a physical objective? It doesn't matter. You can still Receive an abundance of Prosperity, Courage, Love, Forgiveness, Healing — virtually anything — from the Divine Mind itself. This is the boundless source of power I mentioned earlier.

Reception, like Projection, takes practice. While receiving is a passive state, it isn't a condition of surrender. It requires a state of alert awareness. The best description I can give is you enter a mental state of joyful anticipation, as if you're about to meet the most important person in the world, or are about to Receive a wonderful gift, something for which you've waited all your life.

The preparation for Receptive Attraction is much the same as for Projection. The mind must be cleared of obstructive thoughts.

First, enter the Silence, then find the Spiritual Realm of your desire, be it the Realm of Love, Prosperity, Work, Redemption, Cconfidence, Courage, or Health — there's no limit to what you can ask of Divine Mind.

As an example, for love you will enter the Spiritual Realm of Receiving love. You will find the place within you that experiences that joyful, expectant anticipation when you're about to be reunited with someone you love. This sense of anticipation, the desire for union with your lover, creates the powerful magnetism which will fuel the Attractive work.

Next, remember that to be highly effective, your desired affirmation should be compressed into a short Code. For basic love-attraction, your Code might be, *"I'm ready for you, my love, my perfect companion. Come to me."* If you want a better class of friends rather than a sexual partner, your Code might be, *"I'm ready to be loved and admired for who I am. Bring me friends who'll appreciate my wonderful qualities. Come to me, my friends."*

And be alert. This is important. Watch with every nerve you have.

Now draw it in, using your crystal ball as the focal point. From the crystal, claim it. Embrace it. Welcome it. Once you've drank your fill, once you're filled to the brim with it, close it down. I visualize all my Chakra points closing. You may prefer a different way to stop the flow. A hand closing, a door shutting, a tube slowly shrinking.

You know you've got it right if you experience happiness so profound you weep. That surge of power flowing back into you cannot be mistaken for anything else but a "gift-wave" from Divine Mind. It answers "YES."

When you seriously begin studying the art of Attraction, bear in mind that Attraction isn't wish-fulfillment. It's claiming those things that already belong to you. The biggest reason for failure, and why most people lose confidence in their ability to Attract, is because they're trying to Attract the wrong things—things that aren't rightfully theirs.

## WHAT IF YOU FEEL UNABLE TO RECEIVE?

In 1903, the New Thought author Lida A. Churchill wrote a book called *The Magnet*, about the difficulty that people who feel spiritually weak or inept have when trying to Receive blessings. She explains that we are magnetic beings who can Attract all that we desire, but just as magnets may lose their power, we too can become "demagnetized" — especially by engaging in over-anxious thoughts, useless activities, or unkind speech. She urges practitioners to identify the problem and correct it by going into the Silence and affirming, *"I will cease all inharmony in thought or speech ... my every thought, word, and deed shall make me, and keep me, a perfect magnet."*

## WHAT ABOUT NEGATIVE THOUGHT-POWER?

We mentioned earlier that what we take into the Silence comes back to us. We also learned that thoughts, even the random ones that flicker through our subconscious minds, take on a life of their own. When we say "This isn't going to end well," we're opening the door for disaster. When we say, "Amen," we are breathing our hopes into existence. We are, in a sense, doomed to inherit the fruits of our own self-fulfilling curses, and blessed to accept the rewards of our fondest affirmations. There's no Divine fate, reward or retribution for us, that we are the Masters of our Fate, the Captains of our Destiny, the Crafters of the Course of our Lives.

If thoughts have endurance, and if our thoughts come back to us, then yes, we will reap the fruits of our fears, doubts, ill-will, and anxieties. We can't escape the consequences of our own actions. This is the Law of Karma. But there's good news. We don't have to be forever haunted by guilt, or worry that our misdeeds will come back to ruin our happiness.

By Projecting and Attracting positive and powerful thought-waves, the effects of previous negativities are diluted into insignificance. What's important is to begin practicing now, and practice diligently. You can't erase the past, but you can weaken its hold on you.

The best example I can give you is the *Lonaphala Sutta: The Salt Crystal*, from the *Angutara Nikaya*, a collection of the teachings of the Buddha. I've paraphrased it; it's much longer than this brief excerpt:

*The Buddha: "Suppose someone dropped a Salt crystal into a cup of water. Would the water in the cup become salty and unfit to drink?"*

*"Yes, sir. There's only a small amount of water in the cup, because of the Salt crystal, it would be unfit to drink."*

*The Buddha: "Now suppose someone were to drop the Salt crystal into the River Ganges. Would the water in the River Ganges become salty and unfit to drink?"*

*"No, sir. There being a great mass of water in the River Ganges, it would not become salty and unfit to drink."*

*The Buddha: "In the same way, a trifling evil deed done by an unmindful man takes him to hell; and the very same sort of trifling deed done by a mindful man is experienced in the here and now, and for the most part barely appears for a moment."*

## HOW DO OUR THOUGHTS INFLUENCE OUR REALITY?

Exponents of New Thought have written a great deal about the theoretical underpinnings of how something as seemingly vapourous as a thought can shake the concrete foundations of the real world. As noted, some New Thought authors were religious and some were secular. They agreed on how to benefit from the application of affirmations, but when it came to causal principles, the religious authors chose Divine Mind or God as their standpoint and the secularists chose Science. God, I think, is a concept we can all understand. Science may take a bit more explaining.

William Walker Atkinson, a prolific secular New Thought author who published under a hatful of pen names, theorized in *Practical Mental Influence* (1908) that thoughts, like electricity, light, and magnetism, are comprised of "waves," and like all waves, are propagated according to the strength of the sender. To Atkinson, thought-waves were a measurable scientific phenomenon that interact with the natural world.

Atkinson stated that thought-waves emanating from one individual are attracted to similar thought-waves of others, joining with them and creating an attractive force that draws in more similarly-charged thought-waves, until the similar thought-waves of numerous individuals combine to generate enormous waves of power. There is nothing magical or supernatural about this process, according to Atkinson, who appealed to reason, common sense, and hard science, proposing that reality, on the most fundamental level, consists of waves, and therefore can be influenced and shaped by a sufficiently powerful Projection of thought-power.

When we read this, despite the dated science, we find quite a bit of solid reasoning. In the early 20th century, scientists were feeling their way toward quantum theory, so the description of atoms and particles as "waves" was quite in line, and the idea that thought could influence reality wasn't that far removed from the edgier scientific thinking that was emerging at the time.

Since Einstein's Theory of Relativity stated that reality is comprised of space/time events and how these events relate to each other, objects were no longer static events, but activities. There can't be an apple, for example, without all the activities necessary to bring an apple into existence. An apple is an activity, something that is being an apple, as opposed to the table upon which it sits — which is busy being a table. Everything in the universe is a process, constantly in a state of flux and motion, relative to everything else.

Quantum mechanics goes further and claims that these activities, on the very tiny scale, occur as waves of indeterminate nature, which only become determined upon observation. In other words, the act of observation determines the final state of the "object." It could be said that observation is the same as thinking; observation has a direct effect on reality. This is one version of the Copenhagen interpretation of quantum theory, proposed in the late 1920s by Niels Bohr and Werner Heisenberg, but apparently anticipated, albeit indirectly, by New Thought authors!

There are different kinds of thought-waves, according to Atkinson. There are those emanated from everyone, unconsciously and "without purpose," which, he says, have little effect. Others have great force and travel far, with a great deal of influence. Still others are directed purposefully toward specific individuals or places for specific reasons. And finally, there are those thought-waves which are sent out with great force and purpose, but instead of being sent toward any person or location, swirl around in a great vortex, with the intention of influencing everyone with whom they come in contact.

Like other vibratory energies, thought-waves don't dissipate immediately, but can linger for a very long time even after the thinker has stopped sending — and even in some cases, after the thinker has passed away. If you think about buildings that still contain psychic residue, a "feeling" of strong emotional force, you get the idea. Light from stars long dead still reaches the Earth after millennia. If a thought-wave is powerful enough, there's no reason why it can't propagate with equal force, and have equal endurance.

If you can, imagine innumerable bursts of thoughts attracting other thoughts, radiating throughout the fabric of space and time, gathering power over uncountable eons, building, growing, becoming more complex — a vast conscious network connecting mind with mind. If you can catch a glimmer of that idea, you have a non-mystical, physical model for "Divine Mind" as the sum cumulative total of the collective thought-waves radiated by every conscious being in the universe; every being who is alive now, who has ever lived, and perhaps, those who wait to be born. What an unimaginably vast storehouse of creative power!

Religious New Thought authors like Ernest Holmes (1887 - 1960) saw a different principle behind the proven efficacy of thought-power. Wrote Holmes in 1934, *"The hand that gives is the hand of God, and the eye that sees is the eye of God. In each other, through each other, we contact God."*

The choice of theory — religious or secular — is yours to make, of course.

# THE FOURTH BRANCH OF CRYSTAL GAZING: THE TRANSFORMATIVE BRANCH: CRYSTAL MAGIC OR HEALING

That crystals have healing properties is no news to most people, but the use of crystal balls for healing work is a unique branch of crystallomancy pioneered by Mr. Conlin.

If you use spheres of crystalline materials such as Quartz, Hematite, Obsidian, and other stones known for their natural healing qualities, your Projections are naturally enhanced by the properties of the mineral you are working with. Projecting healing thoughts through a healing crystal heterodynes the two energies into a stronger waveform.

Healing with a crystal ball can be performed on yourself, another person nearby or at a far distance, or on all of humanity at once. It's really quite a wonderful practice, and unlimited in both scope and power.

First, clear your mind of any negative thoughts. Mr. Conlin, like all advocates of New Thought theory, tells us that thoughts manifest in daily experience. If you fill your mind with obsessive thoughts of disease, these thoughts will surely manifest as actual illness. Mr. Conlin advises to never read about sickness or symptoms of sickness, but to always think *"I am strong, healthy, filled with power and vitality."* These are the thoughts and feelings upon which you focus your total attention, and which you'll Project into your crystal.

Next, go into the Silence and Project these curative thoughts into your crystal ball. Fill the orb with these strong, happy thoughts of wellness and send them toward your target. Radiate these thoughts in every direction, because crystal Projection is extremely powerful.

## HEALTHY MIND = HEALTHY BODY

The mind holds the key to all success and happiness in life, so it's no news that mental states have a powerful effect on our physical health.

It's well known that stress, anger, depression, and grief have measurable and lasting negative effects on the body. Studies have shown that depressed physiological states respond immediately to the simple act of smiling. Isn't this incredible? Simply by smiling, we trigger a beneficial physiological response, releasing endorphins and other mood-enhancing chemicals.

## MANAGING THE MIND-BODY CONNECTION

There are two components to emotions: mental and physical. If you doubt this, experience it for yourself. Love, for example, is often accompanied by pleasurable physical feelings in the abdominal region. Fear, especially terror, is often felt as a loosening of the muscles in the lower diaphragm. Anger is often felt as a tightening in the upper chest. We speak of the "warm glow" of contentment, "icy fear," "hot rage," etc.

Pain also has a double component, consisting of both mental and physical discomfort. When we experience physical pain, we're likely to simultaneously suffer anxiety, fear, stress, or anger. Pain-reduction techniques consist mainly of quieting the emotional reactions to pain, allowing the mind to distance and dissociate from the physical sensations. Another approach, advocated by Buddhist practitioners, is to replace the feelings of fear and anxiety with more positive mental states of compassion and healing. What this tells us is that the mind-body connection is a direct circuit to overall well-being.

The techniques are simple. First, realize there is a perfectly healthy YOU already present in the Mind's Eye of the Universal Consciousness. All you have to do is connect with this image and draw it into yourself. Imagine this perfect, healthy, powerful YOU, connect with it, and possess it as your own. It is yours — it's YOU.

Next, trigger the body's own natural healing mechanism by cultivating an attitude of joyful expectancy, anticipation, and faith that healing is not only possible, but inevitable. You will become the personification of the perfect, healthy YOU. Healing WILL occur! If there is a specific body part which requires healing, focus your attention on it, visualizing it whole, healthy and functional. Anticipate with joyous heart and mind the healing which is occurring right now! Allow the body-mind connection to do its work. The Laws of Attraction and Correspondence match the thought with the reality.

Finally, New Thought teaches that healthy thoughts lead to a healthy body — but it does not forbid you to see a doctor or force you to refuse medication that has been prescribed for you. Your doctor and pharmacist also intend to heal you — so Project a Code to attract their help!

I can tell you from personal experience that these techniques shorten recovery time from major surgery significantly, boost the immune system, help medications work faster, and shorten the course of infectious diseases.

## THINK YOURSELF WELL!

If you're healing yourself, remember that there is a healthy, strong You existing in the Divine Mind. You will be able to connect with this image of Yourself — your Spiritual Twin — and dwell there in the Silence. Attract energy from this powerful You into your crystal ball, and let the crystal radiate the healing rays. Bask in the rays, as you would under a sun lamp. If you're healing a particular part of the body, hold the crystal near it, or roll the crystal over the afflicted body part. My technique is to roll the ball in small circles between the palm and the body, like kneading clay, or roll it in long strokes along the muscle paths.

When you begin working with differently-tinted glass crystal balls you'll be surprised to notice that each coloured ball has a different feel against the skin. Lavender feels soft, for example, as if it's covered with lotion, while Amber feels wet and cool, and Black feels wet and icy, like an ice cube.

These same techniques can be used with natural stones like Quartz, Jasper, Citrine, or Amethyst. Certain crystals are particularly effective for specific conditions, and we'll be discussing this more in subsequent chapters.

If you're a crystal worker and learn crystal ball techniques, these can be integrated into your work for clients with remarkable results. Charge your crystals by attracting healing power into them before putting them to work at a healing session, and see how much stronger your work becomes.

## PRACTICE PRACTICE PRACTICE

Set aside time every day for practice in the Four Branches of Crystal Gazing. My suggestion is that your curriculum look something like this:

**1. Meditation**
**2. Going into the Silence**
**3. Projection or Sending**
**4. Reception or Attraction**
**5. Healing or Transformation**
**6. Scrying or Seership**

In contrast to Mr. Conlin's plan, I place the study of Scrying as the last of the Four Branches, because for many people it is so difficult to master.

# CHAPTER SIX
## MEDITATION, ENLIGHTENMENT, AND SLEEPING SERPENTS

In his book *Crystal Gazing,* Mr. Conlin describes concentration exercises which resemble many traditional meditation techniques. I too think that meditation is an invaluable skill for developing proficiency in Seership, Projection, Reception, and Healing, and that any effort you dedicate to mastering meditative absorption will earn you tremendous returns.

Always concise and to the point, he taught a basic yet excellent method of meditation, namely, holding a palm-ball sized crystal ball in your hand while fixing your attention upon it for five minutes. Speaking from evident experience, he also described the unexpected difficulties involved in accomplishing this seemingly simple task. The mind and eye wander from the object of attention, and much practice must be invested to successfully master the degree of concentration required. Anyone who's ever started a meditation practice can relate to this.

As a second exercise, Mr. Conlin taught something that will be familiar to those of you who are familiar with Hatha Yoga and the asanas or bodily positions it teaches: He told students to refine their ability to sit in one position for six minutes as a time, observing the body's smallest movements.

Meditation is like everything else in life: the benefits you Receive are proportional to the efforts you invest. Many people meditate simply for relaxation, and that is what they accomplish. However, a meditation practice can bear further fruits. In my opinion, meditation is probably the single most important spiritual skill you can learn. Mastery of meditative absorption provides you greater sensitivity to spiritual assault from outside forces, more awareness of signals and cues people give off (allowing you to distinguish friend from foe), and you'll strengthen the mind's innate abilities to rid itself of negative tendencies and influences.

Meditation isn't hard to master, and there are many traditional and cultural forms of it. You may already know how to meditate. If so, I urge you to practice regularly. If you aren't familiar with meditation, don't worry. It's easy to learn, and all it takes is practice. The more you do it, the better you become.

Read Mr. Conlin's instructions on meditation in this book:
- **Crystal Gazing: Lessons and Instructions in Silent Influence With the Crystal by C. Alexander**

## PREPARING TO MEDITATE

To begin, find a quiet room, and turn off your cell phone. You need a timer. If you're just starting out, I recommend to set it for no longer than five minutes. Gradually increase your time until you mediate for twenty minutes a sitting. Sit in a comfortable, balanced position, and don't strain to sit ramrod straight.

During meditation you're going to spend a lot of time alone with yourself in your head, so it's important that your head is a good place to reside. Close your eyes and say to yourself, *"I'm happy, cherished, and loved. I love myself most of all."* I know this may be contrary to what most of us have been taught, but it isn't possible to love others unless you love yourself. Unhappy people cannot wish happiness for others. You may do so half-heartedly, but if you lack true conviction, you'll find sneaky little ways to punish yourself, and eventually everyone else.

Next, reflect on where and how to find this elusive happiness. It doesn't take long to realize we won't find it in the past. The past is full of unreliable memories and many of them are bad. The future is also unreliable. The only time and place where we have any real power of decision is here and now — but even in the here and now, we have to practice discernment. Not everything around us is dependable. If we try to base our happiness on things that change — sights, sounds, sensations in general, people and things outside — we're setting ourselves up for disappointment. This is simply repeating the past.

The logical conclusion is that true happiness has to be sought within ourselves. Meditation is a search to find a place in the mind where you can't be moved; something solid, unchanging, a place where nothing bad can touch you; no hex, jinx, or curse can reach you, not even death can find you.

To locate this place we need stepping stones. The first step is to cultivate happiness for ourselves. The second is to Project that happiness to everyone else. We do this through identification with every living thing. Tell yourself: *"Everyone, no matter who you are, no matter what you've done to me in the past, I hope you find true happiness."*

Why is this necessary? Because if you don't cultivate loving-kindness, you'll carry negativity into meditation, and that's what you'll find when you look inside yourself. You won't be able to locate that solid, peaceful spot. So make a conscious effort to love yourself and then Project that feeling of love to everyone else. When you've filled your mind with loving-kindness, you're ready to begin meditation.

## CHOOSING A FORM OF MEDITATION

There are so many models of meditation that I would have to write a very large book to describe them all. People of every culture from every time have had something to say on the subject. Meditation is advocated to reduce anxiety, break drug abuse, strengthen concentration, or put an end to restless thoughts. To some, it is a sweat-free path to relaxation, to others, it is a first step on the road to Enlightenment. And what is Enlightenment? Some religions define it as freedom from reincarnation — but if reincarnation is not included in the cosmology of your religion, it may simply mean a way to gain clear insight into your problems. There are even those who say that although meditation will not drive you crazy, certain forms of spiritual awakening may be mistaken for acute psychosis by psychiatric professionals who are unfamiliar with them. In other words, they caution that to the uninformed, Enlightenment may be indistinguishable from madness!

There are many techniques of meditation. Here is a brief list of forms, and until I write that book, you can look them up on the internet:

- **Anapanasati (Buddhist):** Mindfulness of the breath and breathing.
- **Atma Vichara (Ramana Maharshi):** Self-Enquiry; "Who Am I?"
- **Contemplative Meditation (Christian):** Focus on portions of the Bible.
- **Guided Meditation (Modern):** Scripted instructions in visualization.
- **Hatha Yoga (Hindu):** Holding the body in asanas or sacred postures.
- **Kundalini Yoga (Hindu):** Raising powerful serpent-energy up the spine.
- **Mantra Meditation (Hindu):** Focus on a sacred sound or mantra.
- **Merkabah Meditation (Jewish):** Visualization of the light of God.
- **Nada Yoga (Vedic):** Observation of sound, from external to internal.
- **Tantra (Hindu):** A wide range of methods, including meditation on sex.
- **Taoist Meditation (Chinese):** Focus on breath and visualization.
- **Transcendental Meditation:** A modern take on Mantra Meditation.
- **Trataka (Hindu):** Meditation on a scared image called a yantra.
- **Vipassana (Theravada Buddhist):** Mindfulness of the breath.
- **Zazen (Japanese Buddhist):** Sitting, observing the breath, nonthinking.

Nothing you read can take the place of a qualified instructor. If you plan to begin a meditation practice, I advise you find a teacher to guide you.

# CHAPTER SEVEN
# CHAKRAS AND OTHER ENERGY FIELDS

Some time ago I became interested in what role, if any, the Chakra played in crystal ball work. As it turns out, quite a significant one.

To begin, Chakra, which means "wheel" or "disk," is a Hindu concept. A Chakra is an energy node or vortex located along the central channel of the etheric body. Chakras are generally depicted as circular objects with many petals. In Tibetan Buddhism, the "circle" being referred to has dual meaning, as the practitioner reflects on the circle of existence and rebirth.

Depending on the cultural system, there can be as many as several thousand Chakras or as few as three, all contained within the etheric, or "subtle" body. Regardless of this disparity regarding the number of Chakras, all schools agree that the Chakras exhibit certain commonalities:

- **Chakras are energy pools, nodes, wheels, disks, or vortices.**
- **Chakras have "petals."**
- **Chakras are located along the central axis or channel of the body.**
- **Chakras are usually associated with mantras or sacred sounds.**
- **Chakras can be felt, controlled, and developed with practice.**
- **Chakras are associated with psychological traits, emotional qualities, and — conveniently for crystal workers — with colours.**

The purpose of the Chakra is complex. One function is to help filter how we experience the world, and perhaps even store our responses to these various experiences. If the Chakra is truly an energy vortex, it is a powerful whirlpool that draws in emotional energy from our environment and doesn't allow it to escape. This could explain why we harbour positive, and unfortunately, negative emotions for a long time after a powerful experience.

Another function of the Chakra is to act as a "gate," allowing certain types of experiential energy into our awareness according to the Chakra's specific function. For example, someone with a low-functioning or "blocked" Heart Chakra might have difficulty experiencing love, and someone with a blocked Root Chakra might seem lost and unable to fend for themselves.

Western yogic tradition, derived from Hindu yoga, identifies seven Chakras and associates each with a specific colour. These seven Chakras are located in alignment from the base of the spine to the top of the head.

# WHERE THE CHAKRAS ARE LOCATED

1. **The Root Chakra** (Red) is located at the base of the spine. Issues of sexuality, survival, security, food, shelter, and autonomy are seated there.
2. **The Sacral Chakra** (Orange) is located just below the navel. It relates to anger, violence, creativity, new experiences, and how we connect to others.
3. **The Solar Plexus Chakra** (Yellow) is at the pit of the stomach, and it is related to confidence, mastery, personal power, and self-esteem.
4. **The Heart Chakra** (Green or Pink) is located in the mid-chest. It is related to love, compassion, and empathy. Tibetan Buddhists believe this Chakra carries our consciousness into the next existence.

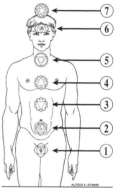

5. **The Throat Chakra** (Light Blue) is located in the throat. It relates to communication, self-expression, and the ability to speak the truth.
6. **The Third Eye Chakra** (Dark Blue) is located on the forehead, above and between the eyes. It relates to psychism, intellectuality, focus, clarity, imagination, wisdom, and decision-making.
7. **The Crown Chakra** (Violet) is located at the top of the head. It is the spiritual focus of our sense of beauty, higher wisdom, illumination, transcendence, enlightenment, and spirituality.

In addition, some practitioners recognize three Chakras outside the body:

8. **The Soul Chakra** is located just above the head, and is the connection to creation, Nature, and the Creator.
9. **The Spirit Chakra** is a Universal Chakra shared by all living things, located outside of time and space, and can only be attained by ascending the highest levels of consciousness. It is union with the Godhead.
10. **The Earth Chakra** is below the feet. It connects to the Earth, grounds the individual, discharges excess energy, stabilizes, and draws determination.

There are hundreds more secondary Chakras throughout the body, but we'll limit our focus to the major seven plus the three non-body Chakras and show how they can enhance our work with crystals and crystal balls.

## WHAT IS A CHAKRA IMBALANCE?

The seven major Chakras located throughout the body are each said to relate in some way to our mental and emotional strengths. Imbalances in these Chakras can indicate (or as some people believe, even cause) physical and emotional issues. These small energy points or vortices along the central channel of the body act as filters or gates of experience. If these filters are not working properly, our experience of reality can be distorted. Furthermore, both emotional and physical symptoms can arise from under-active, over-active, or otherwise malfunctioning Chakras.

Diagnosing whether a Chakra is over-active or under-active is fairly simple. There are specific symptoms associated with the physical and emotional area governed by each Chakra. Usually more than one Chakra will be out of tune. When any Chakra is over-active or under-active—or completely blocked — the other Chakras may try to overcompensate. Therefore, Chakra balancing treatments may be needed for several Chakra points, or all of them.

Our spiritual, emotional and physical states are closely interrelated, and what we experience on one level affects all levels. It's a recognized fact that emotional stress can affect health. But it runs much deeper than that. Imbalances in spiritual, emotional or physical expression can manifest in aches, mysterious illnesses, mental disorders, phobias, nightmares, and all kinds of problems. Many energy workers believe that balancing or realigning the Chakras can alleviate some of these problems.

Obviously, if you suffer from psychological or medical conditions, you must first consult the proper professionals. However, balancing your Chakras may be helpful as an ancillary or supportive treatment along with more conventional therapy.

There are a number of ways to heal and realign Chakras. Treatments involving diet, aromatherapy, meditation, massage, reiki, and essential oils have been used with good results. Crystals have also played an important role in balancing or realigning Chakras, which is very interesting when considering a possible link between crystals, Chakras, and the Fourth Branch of Crystal Gazing, which concerns itself with Transformation and Healing.

Before we prescribe crystals for Chakra-healing, however, we need to learn how to diagnose which Chakra or Chakras are in need of help.

## COMMON ISSUES RELATED TO EACH CHAKRA

• **Root Chakra imbalances** can produce problems in the legs and feet, knees, lower back, lower digestive system, immune system, and genitals.
  • **Under-active Root Chakra** produces emotional problems such as insecurities involving money, shelter, trust, and security.
  • **Over-active Root Chakra** produces emotional problems such as over-spending, greed, gambling addiction, inappropriate need for others to rely on you, "rambling man" syndrome, arrogance, and a sense of rootlessness.
  • **Balancing this Chakra** helps with self-confidence and the feeling of being rooted and grounded.

• **Sacral Chakra imbalances** include sexual and reproductive issues, urinary problems, and kidney dysfunctions, hip, pelvic, and low back pain.
  • **Under-active Sacral Chakra** produces emotional problems, including difficulty committing to relationships, expressing feelings, or acting spontaneously. It can also lead to blocked creativity; inability to experience pleasure; sexual hang-ups; fears of impotence and betrayal; and addictions.
  • **Over-active Sacral Chakra** can produce emotional issues involving hypersexuality, stubbornness, dogmatic inflexibility, engaging in risky or dangerous activities, obsessive behaviours.
  • **Balancing this Chakra** brings the ability to take acceptable risks, be creative, stay committed to a course of action, and becoming capable of passionate, expressive relationships.

• **Solar Plexus Chakra imbalances** include digestive problems, liver, stomach, pancreas, gallbladder, colon issues. Sometimes it can contribute to high blood pressure and diabetes.
  • **Under-active Solar Plexus Chakra** exacerbates emotional problems such as low self-esteem, fear of rejection, and feelings of alienation.
  • **Over-active Solar Plexus Chakra** can lead to grandiose ideation, over-inflated ego, and boundary issues.
  • **Balancing this Chakra** means that self-esteem is raised and self-acceptance is restored to health. Feelings of self-control and assertiveness become easier.

- **Heart Chakra imbalances** include asthma and other lung problems, heart disease, breast, upper back, shoulder, arm and wrist problems.
  - **Under-active Heart Chakra** relates to emotional issues that include codependency, jealousy, anger, passive-aggressiveness, and fears of abandonment.
  - **Over-active Heart Chakra** can cause "love-too-much" syndrome, painful compassion, and hyper-empathy.
  - **Balancing this Chakra** brings feelings of happiness, gratitude, love, and trust are powerful and consistent.

- **Throat Chakra imbalances** include sore throat and laryngitis, ear infections, teeth grinding (especially TMJ), thyroid problems.
  - **Under-active Throat Chakra** can include communication problems, especially speaking the truth.
  - **Over-active Throat Chakra** can include talking too much, "over disclosure" inability to hold onto secrets, gossiping and rumour-mongering, and, oddly enough, talking in your sleep.
  - **Balancing this Chakra** allows words to flow freely; speech is helpful and truthful, and communication is clear.

- **Third Eye Chakra imbalances** include headaches, sinus problems, eyestrain, and loss of hearing.
  - **Under-active Third Eye Chakra** can incline one to moodiness, a tendency to isolate, and narcissism.
  - **Under-active Third Eye Chakra** can lead to hallucinations, over-analysis, fantasy-prone thinking and over-active imagination.
  - **Balancing this Chakra** brings wisdom, clear-thinking, and insight.

- **Crown Chakra imbalances** include depression, mental fogginess, delusions, sensitivity to light and sound.
  - **Under-active Crown Chakra** can bring about prejudice, religious or political extremism, intolerance, rigid thinking of all kinds.
  - **Under-active Crown Chakra** can lead to spontaneous spiritual experiences, anhedonia, asocial behaviour, and disillusionment with people and society.
  - **Balancing this Chakra** allows a more tolerant, open-minded attitude to emerge and helps develop a well-adjusted social attitude.

# BALANCING THE CHAKRAS WITH CRYSTALS

Specific crystals are believed to harmonize with each Chakra, and these crystals are usually paired to the Chakra by colour. Furthermore, since each Chakra harmonizes with a different colour, this type of work also lends itself to experimentation by those who work with tinted glass crystal balls. Each Chakra is associated with a particular colour. When in doubt what stones to use, match the colour of the stone with the colour associated with the Chakra. Here is a handy list of Chakras and crystals related to them.

- **Earth Chakra:** Use black and brown stones such as Mahogany Obsidian, Onyx, Lodestone, Hematite, Magnetite, Moqui Marbles, Flint, or dark, smooth River Rocks. Work with a black glass ball.
- **Root Chakra:** Use red and black stones such as Ruby, Red Jasper, Onyx, Garnet, Obsidian, Hematite, or Fire Agate. Work with a red glass ball.
- **Sacral Chakra:** Use orange stones such as Carnelian, Amber, Jasper, Hyacinth, Tiger's Eye, Imperial Topaz, Cinnamon Aventurine, Orange Calcite, or Orange Sapphire. Work with an amber or orange glass ball.
- **Solar Plexus Chakra:** Use yellow stones such as Heliodor, Sunstone, Lemon Quartz, or Citrine, or chatoyant yellow Apatite, Chrysoberyl, or Sillimanite Cat's-Eyes. Work with a yellow or amber glass ball.
- **Heart Chakra:** Use green or pink stones such as Jade, Moss Agate, Moldavite, Pink Manganocalcite, Rose Quartz, Bloodstone, Ruby in Fuchsite, or Unakite. Work with a green or pink glass ball.
- **Throat Chakra:** Use light blue stones such as Aquamarine, Lapis Lazuli, Sapphire, Shattuckite, Amazonite, Larimar, Turquoise, Topaz, Blue Kyanite, or Blue Lace Agate. Work with an aqua-blue glass ball.
- **Third Eye Chakra:** Use deep blue, purple, and indigo crystals such as Purple Kyanite, Purple Fluorite, Kunzite, Tanzanite, or Purple Apatite. Work with an indigo or deep blue glass ball.
- **Crown Chakra:** Use violet stones like Amethyst, Alexandrite, Charoite, Spirit Quartz, and Sugilite; and white stones such as Moonstone, Selenite, Milky Quartz, or White Calcite. Work with a violet glass ball.
- **Soul Chakra:** Use white stones such as Selenite, Moonstone, Milky Quartz, or White Calcite. Work with a clear or white glass ball.
- **Spirit Chakra:** Use clear crystals such as Clear Quartz, or Rock Crystal. Work with a clear glass ball.

## HOW TO BALANCE CHAKRAS WITH STONES ON THE BODY

One way to balance or realign a Chakra is to place a healing crystal near to or over it. For example, if treating the Heart Chakra, you might choose Rose Quartz, Pink Tourmaline, or Bloodstone. Or you might place all three in a ring around the Chakra area.

Crystals used in this work may be faceted gems, tumbles, flat palm stones, natural or carved points, or roughs. Some of the best crystals I've found for Chakra work are flat, smooth, and about an inch to two inches in diameter. These can be placed directly over the Chakras and allowed to rest for a long period without worrying about them rolling off. Obviously, except for the Crown Chakra, this is easiest while lying down.

Sometimes all that's necessary to improve an imbalance is bringing an appropriate crystal near the afflicted Chakra. Other times treatment takes several sessions before the disharmonious Chakra is back in tune. If working for long-term healing, the client may be instructed to buy small jewelry-quality crystal rings, pendants, or beads to wear.

## HOW TO BALANCE CHAKRAS WITH A STONE CHAKRA WAND

If you're serious about Chakra-centered healing work with stones and you hope to explore and develop your practice further, one handy tool you might want to add to your kit is a stone Chakra Wand, which is basically a stone healing wand — plus. Like any stone wand used to draw negative energy away or to radiate out positive energy, it has a long, central core stone such as Jasper or Quartz, a small crystal ball at the back end, and a crystal point at the working end. Remember:

- **To draw negative energy off,** aim the point away from the area.
- **If you're healing a person,** point the wand toward them.
- **Aim the point of the wand toward yourself** only if you're healing yourself or channeling your own personal energy into an afflicted area.

What makes a Chakra Wand so powerful is that along the central core-stone is affixed a metal strip into which are set seven properly-coloured Chakra stones. When using it, you can literally "push the button" with your thumb to signify the Chakra you are healing. The results are amazing.

## HOW TO BALANCE CHAKRAS WITH A CHAKRA BRACELET

A valuable tool for balancing the Chakras is the Chakra bracelet. There are basically two types — those set with a single stone, meant to treat imbalances of a specific Chakra, and those made with seven stones, one for each of the seven bodily Chakras. Additionally, some Seven-Chakra bracelets are cleverly made to unhook and provide the wearer with a handy Clear Quartz pendulum for answers to questions.

The Seven-Chakra healing bracelet balances the Chakras by neutralizing negative energy that may have gotten trapped in them, and replacing the negative energy with positive energy specific to each gemstone. To use it, meditate briefly on each of the colours, while holding the corresponding stone bead between your thumb and fingers, much as you would while performing devotionals with a Catholic rosary or an Asian mala.

## CLEARING CHAKRAS WITH A MASSAGE WAND AND BALL

This healing technique was taught to me by my colleague Catherine Yronwode. It employs a matched set of stones, one a smoothly tapered cylindrical stone massage wand, six to eight inches long, and the other a stone sphere of the same material, about three to four inches in diameter.

Yronwode explains that any paired stone massage wand and sphere can be used, but that in her practice, "The best results have come from a Ruby in Fuchsite pair for healing blockages of the Heart Chakra and circulatory system, and a Victorite (Spinel in black Biotite) pair for aligning all of the Chakras from the Root to the Crown." The absolute size of the paired pieces is not too important, but the ball should have greater mass than the wand, because it will be used as a collector.

Have the client stand, sit, or recline at ease. Hold the massage wand in your dominant hand and the ball in the palm of your non-dominant hand. Breathe and center yourself, then slowly and gently draw the wand downward over the affected area, keeping it in soft, continuous contact with the client's skin or thin clothing as you collect negative energy into the wand. At the end of each stroke, lift the tip of the wand and discharge it by tapping it firmly onto the ball, which will collect and store the negative energy. Continue to use the stone ball as a collector, discharging the wand as you work, then, when the client has left, cleanse and discharge the ball.

# NATURAL STONES OR GLASS BALLS FOR THE CHAKRAS?

What I'm about to say may cause some traditionalists to scream in outrage, but here goes: In my opinion, coloured glass balls may be superior to crystals and stones when working with Chakras. Here's why I think so:

First, I prefer a ball over a rough or tumbled crystal due to the round shape, rolling motion, and constant contact of the sphere between your hand and the body. Smooth contact maximizes the healing transfer of energy.

Second, glass balls come in every colour of the spectrum, and if you're going to use crystal balls to balance Chakras you'll need seven two-inch balls, one for each Chakra, plus one black ball to absorb negative energies. If you're a purist, the balls can be turned from costly natural stone. But in my opinion, this may be an artificial distinction. Glass is fused silica, the same as natural Obsidian, and the substances used to tint glass are usually minerals, just as Citrine is Quartz, but with a warm yellow glow due to Iron inclusions.

In any case, to treat an imbalanced Chakra, select the colour ball which harmonizes with the Chakra's colour. Starting at the center of the Chakra, roll the ball gently with your palm over the area in gradually increasing circles. When you feel you've reached the perimeter of the Chakra, reverse directions, and spiral it back in toward the center of the Chakra. Repeat as necessary.

An advanced technique is to Project suggestions via your ball, and then transfer this energy by rolling the ball over an appropriate Chakra. The Projected energy would be in the form of healing and balancing Codes. You might Project into a pink sphere, *"Your heart is open and ready for love and friendship. You're brave and confident in meeting new people and initiating romantic relationships,"* and roll this ball over the Heart Chakra.

The black ball is for detoxification. It serves as an amplified version of the black hen's egg used in folk magical cleansing. If you're not familiar with that use of a hen's egg, the idea is that the egg is rolled all over the body to absorb the negative energies, and then the toxins are then safely discharged. The black ball can act in a similar fashion. Rolling an Obsidian or black glass sphere over Chakra points absorbs all entrapped negative energies. This is a wonderful preliminary cleansing before performing balancing or realigning with coloured crystals.

Finally, for the best of both worlds, combine stones and glass balls. Make a triangle of three appropriate crystals around the Chakra and rest your coloured ball in the center. Send your healing through both ball and stones.

## COLOUR THEORY COMES TO THE CHAKRAS

When you look at an artist's colour wheel, you first notice the primary colours red, yellow, and blue. These colours are called "primary" because they aren't blended from other colours. In theory, primaries are combined to create every other colour. The reason this works is that human colour vision is usually trichromatic. The mixing of coloured light in the eye is different than mixing pigments, but red, yellow, and blue are common primaries when painting, while in printing inks, the primaries are slightly shifted to magenta (process red), yellow, and cyan (process blue). As an aside, in electronic colour systems, the primaries are shifted to red, green, and blue, which is why television fails to convey Nature's full range of yellow-tinged hues.

In between the primary colours are green, orange, and violet. These are called the secondary colours, because they're each composed of two primary colours. Between the secondaries are the tertiary colours — but let's limit our attention to primaries and secondaries.

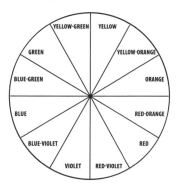

Colours opposite each other on the wheel are complimentary colours. Due to certain optical properties, these colours look very good next to each other. If you place one inside the other, they seem to strobe. Green and red are complimentary, as are orange and blue.

Colours work on subtle levels. They affect energy fields and influence moods. For example, red stimulates aggression, while green soothes and calms. When you begin to think in terms of crystals and Chakras, the idea of complimentary colours becomes very interesting, as crystals may be brought into play when Chakras are over-active or under-active.

## BOOST UNDER-ACTIVE CHAKRAS WITH SIMILAR COLOURS

An under-active Chakra can be treated with a colour-harmonizing stone or glass ball. Massage the area with the stone or ball until the Chakra's energy level feels robust. A severely under-active Chakra should be remediated over the course of several sessions to avoid the risk of overstimulation.

## TAME OVER-ACTIVE CHAKRAS WITH OPPOSITE COLOURS

Sometimes a Chakra is hyper-active, drawing in too much experiential energy. You want to "cool it down" or even neutralize it. This is where complimentary colour work comes in quite handy.

I know it's common practice to think in terms of treating a Chakra with a stone of like or harmonizing colour; for example, treating the Root Chakra with red stones or the Sacral Chakra with orange stones. The idea is that the stone siphons off the excess energy. In this case you wouldn't "charge" the stone before treatment. You'd begin work with inert stones. There is an elegant simplicity to this theory that makes sense.

However, at the risk of flying in the face of established practice, I might suggest an alternative approach for the treatment of over-active Chakras. Perhaps we could take a look at complimentary colour theory. Complimentary colours neutralize each other. If you blend two compliments, you produce a neutral gray tone. If you want to slow an over-active Chakra, consider massaging it with a stone sphere or glass crystal ball of the complimentary colour.

It's been my experience that Chakra hyperactivity responds rapidly to this treatment, with little carryover to adjacent Chakras. If you wish to try this technique, the complimentary colours and a few suggested crystals for the seven Chakras are contained in this handy list of "opposites":

- **Neutralize Overactive Root Chakra with Green:** Use Aventurine, Moss Agate, Chrysocolla, Malachite, Chrysoprase, or a green glass ball.
- **Neutralize Overactive Sacral Chakra with Blue:** Blue Lace Agate, Sodalite, Blue Tourmaline, Lapis Lazuli, or a blue glass ball.
- **Neutralize Overactive Solar Plexus Chakra with Purple:** Use Amethyst, Purple Agate, Sugilite, Charoite, or a purple glass ball.
- **Neutralize Overactive Heart Chakra with Red:** Use Red Jasper, Ruby, Red Tourmaline, Garnet, Red Coral, or a red glass ball.
- **Neutralize Overactive Throat Chakra with Orange:** Use Carnelian, Orange Calcite, Tiger's Eye, Orange Sapphire, or an amber glass ball.
- **Neutralize Overactive Third Eye Chakra with Yellow:** Use Citrine, Heliodor, Yellow Scapolite, Yellow Sapphire, or a yellow glass ball.
- **Neutralize Overactive Crown Chakra with Pink:** Use Rhodonite. Rose Quartz, Rhodochrosite, or a pink glass ball.

# CHAPTER EIGHT
# THE HIGH PRIEST'S SACRED STONES

In the *Book of Exodus* of the Jewish Bible or Christian Old Testament, a remarkable array of twelve sacred stones is described. It is known as the High Priest Aaron's Breastplate, the Breastplate of Judgement, or the Hoshen.

As described, the gems were each rectangular and no two were alike. Each stone represented one of the twelve tribes of Isræl, and the name of each tribe was engraved on the corresponding stone. Arrayed in three columns and four rows, reading right to left, as Hebrew does, the gold-framed gems were set into a brocade cloth vestment. What's more, they held a secret — behind them was a pocket that held two more, unseen stones, the Urim and Thummim, which were used to bring forth Divine guidance on important questions.

Replicas of the Hoshen are crafted and worn today as magical jewelry by people who wish to tap into ancient Biblical power. The true names of most of the twelve sacred stones have been lost due to shifts in language, but many people have attempted to reconstruct the array.

In this table the Hebrew name for each stone is followed by a rough translation, the tribe's name, and a selection of gems that represent both ancient and modern popular attributions. Remember: the order is right to left!

| | | |
|---|---|---|
| Bareket ("shiny")<br>Zebulon<br>Emerald, Peridot,<br>Chrysoprase | Pitdah ("flashing")<br>Issachar<br>Yellow Topaz<br>Heliodor | Odem ("red")<br>Judah<br>Red Jasper, Ruby,<br>Carnelian, Sard |
| Yahalom ("hard")<br>Gad<br>Zircon, Onyx,<br>Clear Quartz | Sapir ("blue")<br>Naphthali<br>Lapis Lazuli,<br>Sapphire | Nofech ("dark red ")<br>Dan<br>Dark Garnet,<br>Carbuncle |
| Achlama ("strong")<br>Levi<br>Amethyst | Sh'vo ("black")<br>Simeon<br>Black Agate<br>Obsidian | Leshem ("Ligurian")<br>Reuben<br>Amber, Citrine,<br>Orange Jacinth |
| Yaspheh ("Jasper")<br>Benjamin<br>Jasper, Hyacinth,<br>Beryl, Sardonyx | Shoham ("streaky")<br>Joseph<br>Beryl, Cat's Eye,<br>Steaked Onyx | Tarshish ("Tarsian")<br>Asher<br>Blue Topaz, Jacinth,<br>Chrysolite |

# CHAPTER NINE
# BIRTHSTONES AND GEMS OF THE ZODIAC

The custom of assigning a stone to each month dates back a few hundred years. Originally the idea was to keep a set of twelve stones and wear one each month. In time, however, the notion of having one special Birthstone took hold. No one agrees on which stone suits each month. Try these choices:

| | |
|---|---|
| **January** | Garnet |
| **February** | Amethyst, Hyacinth, Moonstone, Pearl |
| **March** | Bloodstone, Jasper, Aquamarine |
| **April** | Diamond, Sapphire, Clear Crystal Quartz |
| **May** | Emerald, Agate, Chrysoprase |
| **June** | Cat's Eye, Turquoise, Agate, Pearl, Moonstone, Alexandrite |
| **July** | Turquoise, Onyx, Ruby, Carnelian, Sapphire |
| **August** | Sardonyx, Carnelian, Moonstone, Topaz, Peridot, Ruby |
| **September** | Chrysolite, Sapphire, Lapis Lazuli, Zircon |
| **October** | Opal, Aquamarine, Pink Tourmaline, Coral |
| **November** | Topaz, Pearl, Citrine, Cat's-Eye |
| **December** | Bloodstone, Ruby, Turquoise, Lapis Lazuli, Zircon, Topaz |

In *The Book of Talismans, Amulets, and Zodiacal Gems*, written in 1915, William Thomas Pavitt and Kate Pavitt presented an extensive list of gems by Zodiac sign. Their well-researched list, still valid today, is as follows:

| | | |
|---|---|---|
| **Aries** | March 22 - April 20 | Bloodstone, Diamond |
| **Taurus** | April 21 - May 21 | Sapphire, Turquoise |
| **Gemini** | May 22 - June 21 | Agate, Chrysoprase |
| **Cancer** | June 21 - July 22 | Emerald, Moonstone, Cat's Eye, Pearl, Selenite |
| **Leo** | July 23 - August 22 | Sardonyx, Amber, Tourmaline, Peridot, Imperial Topaz |
| **Virgo** | August 23 - September 22 | Carnelian, Jade |
| **Libra** | September 23 - October 23 | Opal, Lapis Lazuli, Chrysolite, Coral |
| **Scorpio** | October 24 - November 21 | Beryl, Aquamarine, Carbuncle, Lodestone |
| **Sagittarius** | November 22 - December 21 | White, Yellow, or Pink Topaz |
| **Capricorn** | December 22 - January 21 | Ruby, Malachite, Black Onyx, Jet |
| **Aquarius** | January 21 - February 18 | Garnet, Jacinth, Hyacinth, Zircon |
| **Pisces** | February 19 - March 21 | Amethyst |

# CHAPTER TEN
# TECHNIQUES FOR ADVANCED WORK

Performing Projection and Reception work of any kind, especially work involving Silent Influence, requires enormous energy and emotional resources. Like everything else, from marathon running to harmonica playing, the more you practice the better you become. The one thing in common to any area of expertise is perfecting your technical skills to maximize your results with minimal expenditure of effort.

Be sure you're confident with the fundamentals of Projection and Reception before moving on to this advanced section. Believe me, I know from experience that it's far better to learn something properly the first time than to have to go back and correct bad habits.

## CHAKRA-FUELED PROJECTION WORK

Before attempting the techniques of Chakra-fueled Projection, please review the basics outlined on pages 72 and 73 of this book.

Projection is powered by concentrated will power, developed and refined by practice. Our will is fueled by the force of our desires, emotions, and drives. The origin of our most primal drives is the Root Chakra, and it is the Root Chakra that will serve as the dynamo from which we'll draw power for our work.

We're going to summon energy from the Root Chakra, draw it up to whichever other Chakra is appropriate to the condition, and focus this energy into the crystal ball. Then we'll hurl the energy from the crystal ball toward our target like a projectile ray.

For these exercises you'll construct a stand of three crystals on which your ball will rest. Arrange three crystals or stones in a tight circle, and rest the crystal ball on it. What crystals you use, and what coloured crystal ball, will depend on the type of work or spell you're performing.

The technique itself is simple in concept, but requires practice. In Kundalini yoga, you learn to raise the Kundalini energy from the Root Chakra higher and higher to various other Chakras. We're going to practice the same technique, except once the Root energy is raised to the desired Chakra, we'll Project it into our crystal, and from there, out toward our target. Let's look at a couple of examples:

## A LOVE-DRAWING PROJECTION

Using a pink or light-green crystal ball, or a pink crystal ball resting on a circle of light green crystals such Aventurine, Green Calcite, and Jade, clear your mind of all distracting thoughts. A short period of meditation may be useful for this. Next, go into the Silence, enter the Spiritual Realm of pure Causation, and focus on your intentional Code as explained in previous chapters. If you are seeking new love, your Code for Love Projection might be *"My Love, I sense you out there. I'm searching for you. Find me."*

Once your concentration is focussed on this single intention, summon power from your Root, draw it up to your Heart Chakra, and pour it into your crystal. Fill the crystal with your desire, and hurl it out in every direction. A crystal ball is omni-directional. It flings your thought-power everywhere.

If your target is a specific person, your code might be *"Jim or Jane, we are meant to be. Realize our love is true. Love me as I love you."* Visualize the person clearly, and send your thought-wave out toward the person.

Once your Projection is accomplished, return it to the ball, and draw it from the ball through your Heart Chakra. Cherish the energy until you've fully re-absorbed it. Emerge from the Silence and end your session.

## A PROJECTION FOR CONTROLLING SOMEONE

Assuming you want to use Silent Influence to compel your boss to give you a raise, here is a suggested procedure.

Rest a purple or blue crystal ball on a circle of blue and purple crystals such as Amethyst, Blue Kyanite, and Lapis Lazuli. Clear your mind of all distracting thoughts. A short period of meditation may help. Next, go into the Silence, enter the Spiritual Realm of pure Causation, and focus on the idea of total command. Visualize your boss performing the action you desire of him or her — in this case, giving you a pat on the back along with a hefty raise in pay. Your Code for this Projection might be *"Mr. or Ms. Boss, you know I deserve this raise. You will give it to me, and soon."*

Once you're entirely concentrated on this intention, summon power from your Root, draw it up to your Third Eye Chakra, and pour it into your crystal. Fill the crystal with your desire, and hurl it out in every direction.

Having accomplished your Projection, draw it back into the ball, and from there into yourself through your Third Eye Chakra. End the session by closing your Third Eye, or by placing your crystal aside and emerging from the Silence.

## CHAKRA-ENHANCED RECEPTION WORK

There are two ways to practice Reception. The first is to Project the intention, and then re-absorb it. When you're sending a Projection, part of your mind is also in passive receiving mode. If you're sending thoughts of love, for example, those same thoughts become objects of attraction. All you have to do is mentally seize the thoughts and draw them in.

The second method of Reception is what Mr. Conlin calls "Induction." The Divine Mind is a source of infinite power and abundance from which we can draw anything and everything. The Divine Mind takes in and broadcasts our messages, if we know how to send them. With Inductive Reception work, we enter the Silence and then place ourselves in the Spiritual Realm of what we're asking for. This is also called the area of Pure Causation. Having reached a state of cause, we draw in the object of our desire, filling our crystal with the essence of what we are seeking. Once the crystal is completely filled with energy, we absorb it into ourselves. This energy we draw from the Divine Mind (or from a powerful Sender) is called a gift-wave.

Be careful, though. Reception work is tricky, for just an inexperienced spell-caster may fall in love with a client on whose behalf she is drawing in love, Reception can occur as an unintended by-product of Projection. The rule "What is Projected will also be Received" definitely applies to Chakra work. Chakras are energy whirlpools which draw emotional and spiritual experiences into the body. Projections are powerful emotional experiences, and we naturally absorb some of the energies aroused by such work.

As for what role the Chakra plays in the Receptive process, it's apparently an important one. I don't think we have to "train" our Chakras to absorb particular energies. When we perform Reception work, we naturally filter harmonic energies through the appropriate Chakra-gate. After all, that's one of its several jobs. With that said, rather than leaving the Receptive process to run itself (possibly with varying degrees of efficiency) we can enhance the process with controlled visualization and by use of our crystals.

This is nothing new. As we've seen, yogins have trained and harnessed their Chakras for many centuries, often with the use of crystals. All we're offering is an approach that integrates Mr. Conlin's Crystal Gazing techniques with conventional yogic wisdom.

Here's a sample exercise in intentional Reception:

## A RECEPTION FOR A JOB, CAREER, AND ATTRACTION

This is a complex visualization, involving basic needs (Root Chakra) with independence and self-expression (Solar Plexus Chakra). Fortunately, in practice it's fairly simple.

For career, use a honey-amber crystal, and hold it in your hands or rest it on a ring of Red Jasper, Moss Agate, and Iron Pyrite. Clear your mind, during a period of meditation if necessary, removing all distractions from your environment. Enter the Silence, and formulate your Code. If looking for a job in the creative field, this could be, *"My perfect job, designing events, pleasing your clients, I know your company needs me. I'm coming to you. You WILL recognize I'm what you've been looking for."*

In this case, we're asking for our perfect job, the position reserved just for us. We enter the Silence, place our minds in the Spiritual Realm of that Perfect Job, and become joyfully expectant of receiving it. This aligns our thoughts with the Divine Mind. When the Divine Mind responds with the gift-wave, a mighty surge of power is felt. Draw in the gift-wave through the Sacral Chakra, and push it all the way down to the Root Chakra, then snap the Sacral Chakra closed, lay the crystal aside, and emerge from the Silence.

Use the same procedure for any Reception undertaken. Draw the gift-wave in through the appropriate Chakra, push it to the Root, and end the session. For love work, draw the gift-wave in through the Heart Chakra and push it down to the Root. For eloquence, draw the gift-wave into the Throat Chakra and push it to the Root.

This is the most powerful Reception work you can master. It forms a powerfully-energized circuit between the Root Chakra — the source of our grounding vitality — and the Chakra associated with the goal toward which you're working. It supercharges any Projection or Reception work undertaken, and will lift any aspect of ordinary life to extraordinary levels.

If this isn't a skill worth developing, I don't know what is.

## ADDING ZODIAC OR BIRTH STONES TO THE CHAKRAS

In these exercises in advanced Projection and Reception, I recommended that you rest your crystal ball on a circle of stones related to the appropriate Chakra. If you know the Zodiac sign or birth month of a person to whom you are sending Codes, add "their" stone in the center of your circle, under the ball. At the conclusion, give them the charged-up stone as a gift!

# CHAPTER ELEVEN
## USING CRYSTALS IN SPELLWORK

Mr. Conlin says, in *Personal Lessons, Codes and Instructions for Members of the Crystal Silence League,* that every spell cast, every prayer chanted, every wish made, are attempts to influence the will or thoughts of someone else. This suggests that the great magicians of old were masters of Silent Influence. Once Silent Influence is mastered, there's nothing preventing you from becoming a great magician. But there are conditions.

First, you must be familiar with a tradition of magic in which to work. Silent Influence and crystals will augment your efficacy in brujeria, trolldom, ceremonial magick, stregheria, braucherei, or any other formal or folkloric form of magic, but you need grounding in the practice of magic at the outset.

Second, in this book, I will demonstrate the use of crystals, stones, and minerals as applied to hoodoo, rootwork, or conjure, the African-American tradition of folk magic in which I personally work. So, if you are unfamiliar with it, let me provide a simple definition of its origin and style.

Rootwork is Black American Christian herb magic. It incorporates Biblical and personal prayers in support of powerful alliances with spiritually active herbs, roots, bones, stones, and other curios. These curios may be used as-is, or they may be compounded into products such as oils, candles, incense, sachet powders, and bath crystals, and floor washes for use in magic spells.

Prayer is so central to conjure that when my clients request consultation with their own spellwork, the best advice I can give them is to pray like their head is on fire. It's the power of conviction that sends the work on its way.

For more on the history and practice of hoodoo, see these pages online:

**LuckyMojo.com/hoodoohistory.html**
**LuckyMojo.com/hoodoo.html**
**Southern-Spirits.com**
**HerbMagic.com** (click the individual page for each herb)

Learn more about African-American hoodoo and rootwork in these books:

**"Hoodoo Herb and Root Magic" by Catherine Yronwode**
**"Hoodoo Bible Magic" by Miss Michæle and Prof. C.D. Porterfield**
**"The Black Folder" edited by Catherine Yronwode**
**"Hoodoo Spiritual Baths" by Aura Laforest**
**"Hoodoo Honey and Sugar Spells" by Deacon Millett**
**"The Art of Hoodoo Candle Magic" by Catherine Yronwode**

# MAGIC SPELLS WITH CRYSTALS AND STONES

The following examples show how to incorporate crystals, crystal balls, Silent Influence, and Chakra-powered Projections into spellwork. Start with the simpler examples and move to the more complex ones. Don't be afraid to devise your own variations. Feel free to apply these ideas to your own work.

## UNCROSSING AND PROTECTION SPELL WITH RED JASPER

If you believe, or it has been divined, that you're under crossed conditions, you can make a powerful talisman from Red Jasper. You need:

- A piece of Red Jasper
- A 6" orange candle
- Uncrossing Oil
- Crossroads dirt
- A glass of spring water
- Uncrossing Incense

Mound up the crossroads dirt on a plate and bury the Red Jasper in the soil after dressing it with Uncrossing Oil. Draw a crossroads (an X) in the dirt. Place the orange candle in the center of the X. You may need a candle stand to do this safely. Dress the candle with Uncrossing Oil and light it. As it burns, recite these Bible portions: Psalms 3:3 (*But thou, O Lord, art a shield for me; my glory, and the lifter of my head*), Psalms 70:2 (*Let them be ashamed and confounded that seek after my soul; let them be turned backward, and put into confusion, that desire my hurt*), and Psalms 23:4 (*Yea, though I walk through the valley of the shadow of death, I will fear no evil, for thou art with me*).

Raise power from the Root Chakra to fuel your intention. Since we're working magic, Project from the Third Eye.

Concentrate your intention into a fiery blaze, focus it into the Jasper, and when you feel it build to critical mass, let the power explode from the stone in every direction, sending confusion to your enemies and dispersing any and all oppressive conditions in your immediate vicinity!

Once you've sent the spellwork on its way, let it go. Don't fret over it as the candle burns. After the candle finishes, light the incense, unearth the Jasper, and thoroughly smoke the Jasper in the incense fumes, then rinse it in the spring water. Scatter the dirt to the four directions at the crossroads.

Carry the Jasper talisman with you for protection from negative energies and to ward off any further attempts to jinx, hex, or cross you.

## A LOVE ATTRACTION RITUAL
You will need:

- A Rose Quartz crystal
- A Pink Tourmaline crystal
- Come To Me Oil
- A 6" red candle
- 2 holders for the candles
- Rose petals, either red or pink
- Lovage
- Lavender
- A Pink Manganocalcite crystal
- A pink or lavender crystal ball
- Come To Me Incense
- A 6" pink candle
- A Bible
- An oblong white china serving plate
- Damiana
- A red flannel drawstring mojo bag

### Preparation
Pink Manganocalcite is a fairly expensive stone, and Pink Tourmaline is not cheap. If you're on a budget, use three Rose Quartz crystals.

Dress the stones with Come To Me Oil and arrange them in a triangular pattern, upon which the crystal ball will rest. In the space between the stones place a few rose petals, and a pinch each of Lovage, Damiana, and Lavender. Pray over the herbs while situating them, then set the crystal ball on top.

With a pin or nail, carve on the red candle the name of the person you're trying to attract. Carve your name on the pink candle. Also scratch four horizontal marks down the side of the candles to divide it into five equal sections. This doesn't have to be precise.

Place the red and pink candles in two stands, as far apart as you can on the plate. You're going to perform a moving candle spell, which means that over the course of several days (in this case five) you'll move the candles closer together until the nearly touch. The plate is to catch the melting wax.

Each night you'll recite a portion from the Biblical *Song of Solomon*, so write these out on five slips of paper, one for each night. You'll carry the papers and other items in the mojo bag at the conclusion of the ritual.

This spell uses Silent Influence. Raise power from the Root Chakra, and Project from the Heart Chakra. There will be two moments of Projection:

- When you light the candles and recite from the Bible, you will Project directly from the Heart Chakra.
- When you are to Project your intent from the crystal, first build your concentration to a high vibratory level and direct it into the crystal ball.

## The Five Nights of Ritual

On the first night, dress the candles with Come To Me Oil and as you light them, recite from the Biblical *Song of Solomon*:

*Let him kiss me with the kisses of his mouth! For your love is better than wine; your anointing oils are fragrant; your name is oil poured out; therefore virgins love you. Draw me after you; let us run. The king has brought me into his chambers.*

Send power into your recital from your Heart Chakra, and Project it as you light the candles. Also send power into your crystal and crystal ball arrangement as the candles burn. The pink crystals work together with the crystal ball, heterodyning the power sent into it. This amplifies the Projective force in an extraordinary manner you have to experience to believe.

As the candles burn, go into the Silence, entering the Spiritual Realm of pure Romantic Love. Project your desire into the ball, and from there toward your target. Burn the candles down to the first mark, then snuff them out.

On the second night, move the candles a little closer together, dress them with Come To Me Oil, and recite this verse from the *Song of Solomon:*

*The voice of my beloved! Behold, he comes, leaping over the mountains, bounding over the hills. My beloved is like a gazelle or a young stag. Behold, there he stands behind our wall, gazing through the windows, looking through the lattice.*

While the candles burn, go into the Silence, and repeat your Projections. When the flame burns to the second mark, snuff the candles out.

On the third night, move the candles a little closer together, dress them with Come To Me Oil, and recite this verse from the *Song of Solomon:*

*On my bed by night I sought him whom my soul loves; I sought him, but found him not. I will rise now and go about the city, in the streets and in the squares; I will seek him whom my soul loves. I sought him, but found him not.*

Repeat your crystal ball Projections, let the candles burn to the third mark, and blow them out.

On the fourth night, move the candles closer, dress them again with Come To Me Oil, and recite:

*My beloved has gone down to his garden to the beds of spices, to graze in the gardens and to gather lilies. I am my beloved's and my beloved is mine; he grazes among the lilies.*

Go into the Silence, burn the candles to the fourth mark, and snuff them out. On the fifth and final night, move the candles side by side, dress them for the last time with Come To Me Oil, and as you light them recite:

*Set me as a seal upon your heart, as a seal upon your arm, for love is strong as death, jealousy is fierce as the grave. Its flashes are flashes of fire, the very flame of the Lord.*

Repeat your crystal ball Projections for the last time. Allow the two candles to melt together until extinguished.

Collect the remaining wax, herbs, and stones, bundle them together in the flannel bag, and smoke the bag in Come To Me Incense, as you recite:

*Many waters cannot quench love, neither can floods drown it. If a man offered for love all the wealth of his house, he would be utterly despised.*

Carry the bag as a charm to attract your beloved.

### A PYRITE PROSPERITY BATH
You will need:

- Kosher Salt crystals
- Epsom Salts crystals
- Rock Salt crystals
- Pyrite grit or gravel
- Seven whole Cloves
- A small muslin steeping-bag

Mix the Salt crystals, Pyrite, and Cloves, and place them in the muslin bag. Put it in your bath tub and fill the tub with hot water. The Salts will dissolve. As you bathe, Project the Code, *"The riches of the Earth are mine!"* After the bath, scatter the Pyrite gravel and Cloves around your front door.

## PERSONAL MAGIC: A POCKETFUL OF ROCKS

Some stones, like Citrine or Pyrite, are considered to be "lucky rocks" for everyone, but there are also highly personal stones you can use for your own self-empowerment or to represent any person whom you wish to influence in any way. Here's how to select a magic rock to represent a person.

- If the person's first or last name is the same as a stone's name, use that stone. For instance, if the name is Morgan, use Morganite; if the name is Amber, use Amber. Be creative: Malachi becomes Malachite, Angelina is Angelite, Jada is Jade, Khi is Kyanite, and Lara is Larimar.
- If a name's meaning relates to a stone's name in another language, use it: Peter means "rock," so use a River Rock or a non-gem building stone like Limestone; Catherine means "pure or clear" so use Clear Quartz.
- If a man's name is one of the twelve tribes of Isræl, such as Benjamin or Dan, use a stone from the Breastplate of the High Priest for that tribe; for instance, Benjamin can be Jasper and Dan can be Garnet.
- If you know the person's Zodiac sign, select a stone that symbolizes that sign, such as Carnelian for a Virgo or Ruby for a Capricorn.
- If you know the person's birth month, choose an appropriate birthstone, such as Amethyst for February.
- If the way you want to influence yourself or another person relates to a Chakra, pick a stone of that Chakra. For instance for a career as a singer, use a blue Throat Chakra stone like Aquamarine, and to get elected to office, use a self-esteem boosting Solar Plexus Chakra stone like Citrine.
- If you know nothing about a person, as might be the case if you are trying to influence a stranger, then use Clear Quartz. The "great mimic" of the mineral world, it will take on almost any vibration.

To foster creativity, use natural crystals; to influence someone, choose worked stones shaped by human hands, such as spheres, tumbles, or carvings.

You can select several stones and carry them in a mojo bag. For instance, for the loyal affection of man named Dan Travers who is a Leo born in August, make a mojo containing Garnet (Breastplate), Travertine (surname), Peridot (Zodiac sign), Topaz (birth month), and Rose Quartz (Heart Chakra).

Craft a metaphysical mineral tincture by soaking your chosen stones in alcohol and administering a spoonful daily in beverages or food.

Soak selected stones in perfume or fragranced oil and wear the scent.

## PINK STONE LOVE SPELL WITH A SUGAR OR HONEY JAR

Projection techniques can be practiced with any crystalline substance. Did you know, for example, that sugar is a crystal?

Sugar, honey, and syrup spells are tools for attracting a love partner, or for "sweetening" a specific person who may have neutral or negative feelings for us. These spells are often worked inside of containers, such as bowls, bottles, boxes, or jars into which various herbal, mineral, or animal curios have been added for magical purposes. Personal concerns, the names of the targets, and petition papers are also added to the jar, and a candle may be burned on top of the lid for the duration of the spell.

For this spell, you will need:

- A small red candle
- A small jar with screw-on lid
- A picture of the "target"person
- A Rose Quartz stone
- A Rhodocrosite stone
- A pinch of Cinnamon powder
- A pinch of Ginger powder
- Come To Me Oil
- Sugar or Honey (or a mix of both)
- A picture of yourself
- A Pink Kyanite or Rhodonite stone
- Three dark pink Rose petals
- A pinch of Lavender flowers
- A plate on which to set the jar
- A small personal concern from your target (a hair, fingernail clipping, handwriting, button, fragment of clothing, foot-track dirt, or such)

If you're on a budget, use three Rose Quartz tumbles.

In making a sweet jar, some people will tell you to fill the container halfway with sugar, honey, or a combination of the two, add the magical ingredients, stir, and then cover everything with the rest of the sweetener. However, a much cleaner way to work is to enclose the herbs inside a petition paper. This leaves the sweetener available for use in edible spells and tricks later on — that is, you will be able to use it in cooking and you can actually feed it to the person you are sweetening.

To work in this way, you can start by writing your petition out on a small square of paper and over that sign your name three times. Alternatively, you can write your name and the name of the person you're trying to sweeten on the paper three times, so your names cross each other at right angles, then write your wish in a circle around your interconnected names. This is similar to a Projection Code, and could be as simple as, *"John Smith, you love me and want to be my husband."*

Once the petition is written, fold the herbs and the personal concern into the paper and place it in the jar. For a neat way to fold such a petition paper and keep it sealed in a "seed-packet style" envelope, see the book *Paper In My Shoe* by Catherine Yronwode.

Some workers taste the honey as they put the packet in it, saying, *"Just as this honey tastes sweet to me, so will I become sweet to you, John Smith."* You can say this three times, tasting the sweetener each time, then seal the jar.

Place the pictures of you and your future love on the plate, face to face, as it for were kissing. At this point, according to tradition, you would position the honey jar on the pictures, place the red candle on the jar and let it burn, but I'm going to suggest you try a slight deviation from that.

We've been developing techniques involving sending Projections via crystal spheres through the Divine Mind to various targets for specific goals. I suggest in this case that you use the honey jar as a crystal ball.

Enter the Silence, step into the Realm of Love Causation, and picture yourself with your ideal and true love. Project this desire into the honey jar, and from there into every direction. When you feel the answering gift-wave respond to your Projection, draw it back into the jar. Once the honey jar is filled with energy, place it on the plate directly over your pictures. Arrange the three crystals on the plate around the jar.

Place the red candle on the jar, dress it with Come To Me Oil, and light it. Burn the candle a few minutes every Monday, Wednesday and Friday until it is finished. You may continue adding candles to the jar as long as you like. Eventually the jar may be completely covered in wax. This isn't a problem.

If the spell is successful and you snag your lover, you can deploy the sweetener by cooking with it and feedings it to him or her. A gentle method of disposal is to take the jar to an ant hill, open it, and ask the ants to take the sweetness to all their friends and relatives worldwide. If the spell was unsuccessful, open the jar and wash the remains away in running water.

Spells like this can be used to sweeten a boss, court judge, school bully, or a bank loan officer, but in this case, we worked for love, which is why our choice of candle-dressing oil was Come To Me Oil rather than something like Court Case Oil or Steady Work Oil.

If you are new to sweet jars, learn more on this web page:
**LuckyMojo.com/honeyjar.html by Catherine Yronwode**
Read about every possible kind of sugar and honey spell in this book:
**"Hoodoo Honey and Sugar Spells" by Deacon Millett**

## MONEY SPELL WITH MALACHITE AND CANDLES

Malachite is a wonderful, inexpensive money-drawing stone. Here's an easy and effective spell. You'll need:

- Three pieces of Malachite
- A 2" (33mm) green glass ball
- Wealthy Way Sachet Powder
- Three crumpled dollar bills
- Three small green candles
- Wealthy Way Incense (optional)

Dress the three dollar bills with the Wealthy Way Sachet Powder and crumple them into tight balls. Arrange the three Malachites in a ring, and put the three crumpled bills in the space inside the circle formed by the stones. Place the green glass crystal ball on the stones and bills, which form a small stand. Arrange the three small candles around the crystal ball. If you'd like to enhance this spell, you can burn Wealthy Way Incense.

For the recital of Psalms, you may choose from these:

- Psalms 118:25: *Save now, I beseech thee, O Lord: O Lord, I beseech thee, send now prosperity.*
- Psalms 1:3: *And he shall be like a tree planted by the rivers of water, that bringeth forth his fruit in his season; his leaf also shall not wither; and whatsoever he doeth shall prosper.*

Bring power into your recital up from your Root Chakra, and send it out through the Sacral Chakra as you light the candles and recite the Psalms.

As the candles burn, go into the Silence, entering the Spiritual Realm of Prosperity. Imagine what it would be like to have an abundance of wealth, to have all your bills paid, money to give your friends and family, freedom to do anything you want, to travel or to build an estate, freedom to live the lifestyle you've always dreamed of.

When you know you're dwelling in the Spiritual Realm of Pure Wealth and Prosperity, you're ready to send. Your Code might be: *"I'm ready to claim my power, wealth and prosperity, and the means whereby to achieve it. I'm ready. My abundance is here, I'm claiming it."*

Project from the Sacral Chakra into your crystal ball, and from the ball in every direction. Sustain the Projection for several seconds. Since this is an attraction spell, you won't absorb the power back into yourself, but draw the power back into the crystal ball and leave it there to empower the spell.

## A LODESTONE AND RED CANDLE SPELL FOR NEW LOVE

Cat Yronwode teaches this traditional seven-day hoodoo spell of love:

You will need a pair of large Lodestones (male and female if you are heterosexual; both male or both female if you are homosexual), a packet of Magnetic Sand, a tray or plate (not made of steel or iron), anointing oil, small personal items or paper and ink, and a red candle. A plain offertory candle will do, but a red "Lovers" or red "Bride and Groom" candle are particularly appropriate for drawing a partner of the opposite sex.

Before you begin Lodestone love spells, determine which ends of the Lodestones draw to each other most strongly. Place the Lodestones on the tray, some distance apart, with the attracting ends facing each other. Behind them and between them, forming a triangle, set up the candle.

Next, name the Lodestones: one for you and one for the person you wish to attract. If you can get anything of the person's (a photo, a lock of hair, nail parings), place it beneath the person's Lodestone. Place something similar of yours beneath your Lodestone. If you cannot get such items, write the person's name three times in red ink on one piece of white parchment and your name three times in red ink on another piece of white parchment and place those beneath the respective Lodestones. If you are already having sexual relations with the person you wish to have love you, then you may simply personalize the Lodestones by anointing them with sexual fluids: semen for a "he" stone and vaginal fluids or menstrual blood for a "she" stone.

On the first day, dress the candle with a love-drawing oil, such as Come To Me, Love Me, Follow Me Boy, or Lavender Love Drops. Sprinkle a little of the oil on each Lodestone as well. Light the candle and feed the Lodestones with one-seventh of the Magnetic Sand. Concentrate on your desires. You may also read aloud the *Song of Solomon*, which is in the Bible. Let the candle burn one-seventh of the way down and snuff it.

The next day, move the Lodestones a little closer to each other. Again light the candle and feed the Lodestones with one-seventh of the Magnetic Sand. Concentrate on your desires and read aloud the *Song of Solomon*. Let the candle burn one-seventh of the way down and snuff it.

Continue in this way for seven days until the candle is finished and the Lodestones are touching and are well covered with Magnetic Sand.

When the ritual is done, place the Lodestones, still on their tray, in a safe place where they can continue to draw to each other.

### THREE MAGICAL USES FOR A NATURAL HOLED STONE

Natural holed stones found in a river or by the sea don't often look like much. They are generally grey or tan and do not take on a high shine or polish. However, magically speaking, they are among the most powerfully potent stones known, and can be used in many spells. Here's how:

- **Protection:** Hang a holed stone from a cord by the front door to stop wicked people from entering and to ward off night hags and evil spirits. If you have many doors and windows, you may hang a holed stone by each opening. When a cord breaks and a stone falls, you'll know that it "took a hit" for you. Wash it in Salt water, rehang it, and it will keep right on working to protect the house and all who dwell within. If you want protection while you travel, wear a holed stone on a cord as a necklace.
- **Psychic Visions:** To gain the gift of second sight walk out in Nature on a clear full moon night, sighting the landscape through a holed stone. With practice and luck, you will be able to see Fairies and Nature Spirits.
- **Healing:** Those who are sick should certainly go to a doctor, but many amazing folk magic cures have also been reported by the simple means of rubbing a holed stone over an affected portion of the body.

### HOW TO FIX A GEMSTONE RING FOR SCRYING

Start by selecting a ring in which is set one of the many scrying stones listed on page 42. It should fit comfortably and be well made. Gemstones are powerful in and of themselves, but magicians know that when working with a gem for scrying or divination, you will get faster results if you attune or "fix" the stone to yourself before putting it to use.

For seven days and nights, do not wear the ring on your finger or try to scry with it, but carry it in contact with your skin, talk to it, and sleep with it. Ask it if it has a name, and if it replies, address it by that name.

You may, if you wish, attempt to draw a spirit of divination into your ring. To do so, you must first have contact with that spirit. Burying a piece of jewelry in a grave is one way invite a familiar spirit of the dead to take up residence within. Ceremonially invoking a spirit and commanding or inviting it to dwell in the stone is another ancient method.

After seven days, or after a familiar spirit is brought into the ring, hang it on a cord and test its accuracy by using it as a pendulum. If the answers prove out, the ring is ready to wear n your finger as a scrying stone.

## CONCLUSION

By now I hope you've practiced some of the techniques and tools described in these pages, and seen for yourself how powerfully they can affect your mental and physical states. If nothing else, I hope you've developed a new love and appreciation for the wonderful qualities of stones and crystals, Earth's beautiful gift to us. They truly are marvellous things!

When Mr. Conlin passed into the Silence in 1954, I don't know if he imagined the effect his work would have on future generations—or if he imagined his work would survive him at all. I like to think he's aware of how much he's helped so many people, and how his work has been studied and passed on from Master to Student. Sometimes it seems as if he is still among us, nudging and helping, giving us insights when we need them.

These techniques work. I could fill another book with stories and case histories of people who turned their lives around, who healed themselves, who changed reality, through daily application of crystal Projection. Perhaps one day soon I can tell your story.

# BIBLIOGRAPHY

Atkinson, William Walker (as "Swami Panchadasi") A Course of Advanced Lessons in Clairvoyance and Occult Powers. Advanced Thought Publishing, 1916.

Churchill, Lida A. The Magnet. The New Tide Publishing House, 1903.

Conlin, Claude Alexander (as "C. Alexander"). Crystal Gazing: Lessons and Instructions in Silent Influence With the Crystal. C. Alexander Publishing Co., n.d. (c. 1919). Reprinted by Missionary Independent Spiritual Church, 2012.

Conlin, Claude Alexander (as "C. Alexander"). The Inner Secrets of Psychology Volumes 1-5. C. Alexander Publishing Co., 1924.

Conlin, Claude Alexander (as "C. Alexander"). Personal Lessons, Codes, and Instructions for Members of the Crystal Silence League. C. Alexander Publishing Co, n.d. (c. 1913). Reprinted by Missionary Independent Spiritual Church, 2011.

Conlin, Claude Alexander (as "C. Alexander"). The Projective Branch of Crystal Gazing. C. Alexander Publishing Co., n.d. (c. 1924).

Cunningham, Scott. Cunningham's Encyclopedia of Crystal, Gem, and Metal Magic. Llewellyn, 1996.

Gienger, Michæl. Healing Crystals: The A-Z Guide. Earthdancer, 2005.

Hall, Judy. The Crystal Bible. Walking Stick Press, 2003.

Karpo, Padma. Epitome of the Great Seal. Oxford University, 1958.

Klein, Cornelius, Manual of Mineralogy. John Wiley and Sons, 20th ed., 1985.

Lao Tzu. Tao Te Ching. Edited by D. C. Lau. Penguin, 1963.

Lingpa, Karma. Bardo Thodol (Tibetan Book of the Dead). Oxford University,1927.

Nelson, Robert Alan, (as "Dr. [Korda] Ra Mayne"). Six Lessons in Crystal Gazing. Psychic Science Publishing Co., 1928.

Seward, Professor Alfred Francis. The Art of Crystal Gazing or Secrets of the Crystal Revealed. A.F. Seward & Co., 1920.

Shinn, Florence Scovel. The Wisdom of Florence Scovel Shinn. Start Publishing, 2012.

Simmons, Robert and Ahsian, Naisha. The Book of Stones. North Atlantic Books, 2007.

Yronwode, Catherine, Books About Crystal Gazing and Psychic Scrying Published Prior to 1950. YIPPIE, 2010. http://www.yronwode.org/crystal-gazing-bibliography.html

Yronwode, Catherine. New Thought Bibliography from 1870 - 1970. YIPPIE, 2007. http://www.yronwode.org/new-thought-bibliography.html

Space forbids a complete list of New Thought authors, but these names will get you started. Books by many of these authors remain in print or are available online as free texts.

**Religious New Thought:** Mary Baker Eddy, Emma Curtis Hopkins, Charles Fillmore, Myrtle Fillmore, Malinda Cramer, Annie Rix Militz, Nona L. Brooks, and Ernest Holmes.

**Secular New Thought:** William Walker Atkinson, Claude Alexander Conlin, Napoleon Hill, James Allen, Wallace Wattles, Perry Joseph Green, Lida A. Churchill, Frank Channing Haddock, Edward E. Beals, Orison Swett Marden, Elizabeth Towne, and Thomas Troward.